HIRE TALENT FOR
HIGHER VALUE

HIRE TALENT FOR HIGHER VALUE

**USING MEASURES, MODELS & RECRUITMENT
TECHNIQUES FOR MAXIMUM IMPACT**

Abdulaziz Al Kadi

ISBN: 1523890681
ISBN 13: 9781523890682
Library of Congress Control Number: 2016902604
CreateSpace Independent Publishing Platform
North Charleston, South Carolina

To my parents:
all my knowledge is from you.

To my wife, Bayan, and my girl, Lama:
you are the loves of my life, now and forever.

CONTENTS

ACKNOWLEDGMENTS

I would like to express my sincere gratitude to my colleagues at Al Faisaliah Group for letting me complete this project. I am especially grateful to Faisal Al Arfaj, chief human resources and corporate services officer of Al Faisaliah Group, for your ongoing support and leadership, and for pushing me further than I thought I could go.

I am also grateful to Michael Andrew, chief talent and leadership development officer of Al Faisaliah Group and author of *How to Think Like a CEO and Act Like a Leader*. This project would not have been possible without your endless support and encouragement.

Most of all, I am fully indebted to my friends and family. In one way or another, they supported me, helped me survive all the stress during this project, and never let me give up.

I hope those who are interested in this book find it comprehensive.

CHAPTER 1

Recruiting 101: The Fundamentals of Talent Acquisition

As an introduction to this practical handbook, I will start with the fundamentals of recruiting and talent acquisition. I have decided to define the term *talent* using different perspectives and will provide insights into an effective process of talent acquisition that will assist you in fulfilling your company's overall objectives and gaining a competitive advantage.

This chapter looks at common recruitment practices you might be interested in incorporating into your company's hiring process.

Based on my work experience in recruitment, I will explain advanced hiring techniques using a number of frameworks and hiring models. By utilizing all proven metrics presented in this book, recruiters and human resources (HR) professionals will excel in talent acquisition and hire top-notch talent.

Definition of Talent Acquisition

Talent acquisition (also known as recruitment) is essential to achieve departmental results, gain a competitive advantage, and fulfill a company's overall goals and objectives.

Talent acquisition is basically hiring the most fitting candidate you find in the market to fill a vacant position. This decision of who best fits the position is based on the identified job description and the pay scale. There are several objectives that recruiters and HR professionals use to effectively assess talent:

- matching talent with the role's identified job description (JD)
- evaluating the candidate's technical expertise and know-how
- measuring competencies to hire top-notch talents
- hunting for the best cultural fit
- targeting exceptional behaviors and positive attitudes

Why the Hiring Process Is Necessary

Recruiters and HR professionals look for candidates who can deliver on the required standards of the jobs they are hired to do. This is a shortsighted way to look at the purpose of hiring, though. I prefer to align talent acquisition with the company's vision, goals, and objectives. Then the purpose of hiring becomes to hire candidates who can not only deliver on the jobs—per job descriptions and required skills— but who can also support the company to fulfill short- and long-term objectives.

Are you going to hire winners and reject losers? Yes, you can, but you should have a plan, purpose, and solid process to align your recruitment strategy with the company's vision and goals.

Definition of Talent

The definition of *talent* varies across companies as well as competing markets. There is no one definition that all companies settle on, but a simple definition is "an exceptional individual." An employee is exceptional due to performance, unique competencies, leadership, or any other attribute that adds value to the business. Gallardo-Gallardo, Dries, and Gonzalez-Cruz (2013, 291) offer a definition of talent: "Talent can be considered as a complex amalgam of employees' skills, knowledge, cognitive ability and potential. Employees' values and work preferences are also of major importance."

A Company's Definition of Talent

I highly recommend defining talent based on your business's needs. Talent might be viewed differently in a multinational company than in a local one. Therefore, you should have a clear definition of "talent" that identifies the required skills, characteristics, or competencies you aim to have within your workforce.

Within the frame provided by the definition, there are key factors most companies concentrate on when hiring, assessing, and developing talent—work experience, leadership, know-how, qualifications, attitude, competencies, and cultural fit. See table 1.1 for a comprehensive model of talent definition. A company might compose something like this based on business needs and requirements. The model breaks up talent into three career levels—fresh talent, experienced talent, and senior talent.

Table 1.1.

Fresh talent (New graduate up to two years of experience)	Experienced talent (Three to nine years of experience)	Senior talent (Ten or more years of experience)
❑ Is well-educated, with a degree from a reputable university or equivalent ❑ Graduated with honors; higher grade point average (GPA) is a plus ❑ Has master in business administration (MBA) or other master's degree; earning a professional certification is a plus ❑ Has exceptional communication skills and language fluency ❑ Has mastered required competencies and values ❑ Has extra activities, internships, or training experience ❑ Has flexibility and willingness to relocate ❑ Fits company's culture	❑ Is well-educated, with a degree from a reputable university or equivalent ❑ Has MBA or other master's degree; earning a professional certification is a plus ❑ Has three to nine years of work experience in a reputed company ❑ Has multinational experience ❑ Has exceptional managerial skills ❑ Has mastered required competencies and values ❑ Is able to lead a business with $70 million in revenue ❑ Fits company's culture	❑ Is well-educated, with a degree from a reputable university or equivalent ❑ Has MBA or other master's degree; earning a professional certification is a plus ❑ Has ten years of work experience (minimum) ❑ Has multinational experience ❑ Has multifunctional experience ❑ Has exceptional leadership skills ❑ Has mastered required competencies and values ❑ Is able to lead a business with $120 million in revenue ❑ Fits company's culture

The Five S Recruitment Model

There are five fundamental steps I recommend following to cover all parts of hiring and talent acquisition. I have excluded the workforce planning part, which will be comprehensively reviewed in chapter 3. Man-power planning or workforce forecasting could be assigned to man-power planners who don't practice recruitment. Therefore, as seen in figure 1.1, specifying, searching, screening, short-listing, and selecting are the five *S*'s of this recruitment model. These increase hiring efficiency, improve quality, and help people excel in talent acquisition. A description of each step is outlined below.

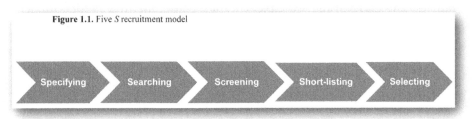

Figure 1.1. Five *S* recruitment model

Specifying Searching Screening Short-listing Selecting

The *specifying* step identifies all job requirements, specifications, and descriptions. What I prefer to do is list all main tasks, competencies, and skills I aim to have within the workforce.

In the *searching* step, search for the talent, and use all the resources you can. At this stage, you will be looking everywhere—job portals, LinkedIn, internal applicants, referrals, and the company's website. Your main plan is to exploit social media, job portals, and referral systems within your company to widen your search scope and identify talent individuals to interview for all vacant positions. You might also announce jobs internally, if internal hiring is a common practice within your company.

When you get to *screening*, you will scan the profiles of your applicants. You can screen people according to their interest in the job and availability for joining. Give yourself some time to review résumés and conduct telephone interviews for rapid screening, in which you initially assess observable competencies such as communication, language fluency, and so on.

Short-listing is the part where you decide who should be in your company's talent pool. You will have to come up with a short list that includes at least two candidates you feel are the closest fits for the job. When short-listing, make sure to send résumés along with your initial assessments of short-listed candidates to concerned departments. Explain why you selected them and what made their profiles unique. Summarize their educational backgrounds, their experiences, and some observations you made during telephone screenings. Table 1.2 shows an example of a short report you might create for each potential talent.

The last step is *selecting*, when you will make the critical decision of which person to hire. The decision will be made after going through specifying, searching, screening, and short-listing. Also, all kinds of assessments have been conducted, including numerical tests, IQ tests, and (most importantly) in-person interviews. You should apply any kind of assessment you view as a solid predictor of success and high performance.

Table 1.2.

Name	Strengths
Mark Lauren	A very mature individual, who demonstrated professional behaviors and unique communication skills. He has solid multinational experience in several companies, such as company XYZ and company XY. He has the expertise required in financial planning and reporting.
Current company	
XYZ	
Current position	
Finance director	
Education and qualifications	Weaknesses
MBA, CFA	No experience in the FMCG industry.
Recommendation	
I highly recommend hiring Mark due to the exceptional technical know-how he showed during the interview. Although there are some areas he needs to develop due to his lack of experience in the FMCG industry, Mark can learn today and apply tomorrow.	

Reference Checks

I don't know why many recruiters overlook or are perhaps not interested in regularly conducting reference checks. This simple, cost-effective tool is one essential practice that can inform your final hiring decision. It gives you feedback on current behaviors and the achievements of your nominated talents.

Recruiters usually spend so much time interviewing candidates and administering verbal, numerical, or cognitive-ability tests to make certain they are hiring the best recruits. All these tests might be used, but still, no one witnesses the performance of your nominated candidate. At this stage, you need to ensure the candidate is who he or she claims to be. You want more evidence and recommendations for your final selected candidate; therefore, you are highly encouraged to conduct reference checks.

- Reference checks are not based on what a candidate is telling you he or she did. It's based on history and real performance.
- You can ask for many references from different backgrounds, which will reveal a candidate's strengths and weaknesses from different angles.
- I view a reference check as an effective, validating approach to confirm any observations you have made during the interview.
- There is no cost associated with reference checks (in most cases).

Always make sure your reference checks are structured in the sense that standard questions are required to be addressed, knowing that many might evaluate candidates based on friendships or personal relations. I highly suggest when conducting reference checks that you focus on leadership, and behaviors, performance or technical knowledge (see table 1.3).

A reference check is one of the most vital recruitment techniques, and it is usually the last step of any hiring process. I totally believe in reference

Table 1.3.

Questions	Comments
How long have you known the candidate?	I recruited John back in 2004 as my insurance manager when I was the GM of company XZ. I have known him for more than ten years, and our paths crossed at regular intervals, so I kept up-to-date on his activities.
Why did the candidate leave?	He left for a better opportunity.
What's your view of the candidate in regard to technical knowledge and performance, leadership, and behaviors?	**Technical knowledge**: He was technically sound with good knowledge of insurance, safety standards, and developments in the field. **Leadership**: He had outstanding leadership abilities. He used this to smoothly manage subfunctions, and he didn't receive any complaints from subordinates. **Behaviors**: He demonstrated positive behaviors and had a high level of integrity and honesty.
What are the candidate's major weaknesses or areas of improvement?	I am not aware of any particular matters I would like to highlight.
Is there any other valuable information you feel might be of relevance about the candidate?	I believe John performs optimally in solving complex problems.
Overall, how would you rate the candidate's performance?	■ Significantly exceeds expectations ❏ Exceeds expectations ❏ Meets expectations ❏ Needs improvement
Name: Adam Smith **Current Position**: CEO	**Date**: 01/01/2016 **Reference check for**: John Smith

checks, and I am confident they lead to better results than other tests, such as psychometric or IQ.

However, I don't recommend asking about the technical knowledge or leadership skills of fresh graduates or entry-level candidates. They are still learning. In other words, it's too early to judge their know-how. The main objectives of entry-level candidates are to increase the learning curve, observe, and acquire leadership skills. You might appraise commitment and attitude or general behaviors, but don't fixate on the technical aspects of a candidate's résumé. These young candidates are just starting their journeys.

The Recruitment Authority Matrix

Deciding who approves a certain task, budget, or project is essential for both the entire organization and any given department. Clarity about duties and accountabilities fosters better communication and results in organized processes, empowerment, and enhanced work efficiency. I highly recommend arranging authorities and approvals within your talent acquisition department. Who approves job descriptions? Who appoints headhunting and executive-search firms? How many approvals are necessary to conduct man-power planning and workforce forecasting?

However, before answering all such questions, you have to scan your company's culture and examine management styles. Does your company have a centralized or decentralized decision-making model? Who are your major players in making recruitment decisions? Who will participate in recruitment during the year? How strong is the relationship between the HR and finance departments? Does your company value work delegation? Do you have an active executive committee? Designing an authority matrix for the recruitment department requires answers to all of the above.

The recruitment authority matrix requires the interaction of other critical players, including the chief financial officer (CFO), chief executive officer (CEO), and perhaps others who work closely with the recruitment department. The bottom line is that you have to align all engaged parties.

Figure 1.2 is an example of a recruitment authority matrix. The matrix explains who should propose and approve each recruitment activity. You will notice, for example, a recruitment representative, or recruiter, proposes creating job descriptions, which requires a hiring manager and a department head to grant approvals. On the other hand, allocating compensation for new hires requires approval from both the chief human resources officer (CHRO) and CEO.

There is no one matrix that will precisely fit all companies. The organization's hierarchy, size, span of control, and centralization of decisions and other associated factors have to be reviewed broadly before endorsing the authority matrix of the recruitment department.

Figure 1.2.

Authority Matrix—Recruitment and Hiring	Executive Committee	CEO	CFO	Dept. Heads	CHRO	Hiring Manager	Recruiter
Hiring Junior Positions (ranging from level one to level five)				Approve		Approve	Propose
Hiring Managerial or Senior Positions				Approve	Approve	Propose	
Setting Grades of New Hires					Approve	Propose	
Creating Job Descriptions				Approve		Approve	Propose
Appointing Headhunters and Executive Search Firms					Approve	Propose	
Allocating Compensation of New Hires		Approve			Approve	Propose	
Man-Power Planning and Forecasting	Approve	Approve	Approve	Approve	Approve	Propose	

● Approve   ▲ Propose

Advice to Recruiters: SMART Recruiting

Most people are aware of SMART (specific, measurable, aligned, realistic, and time-framed) techniques for setting goals and objectives. These ideas are applicable to recruitment and talent acquisition, too. The SMART technique is more fully described in Bogardus's (2009) study guide for HR professionals, but here is a brief summary:

- *Specific*: Specify your job description (JD) and explain tasks, responsibilities, and duties required for the job. Job specifications are required, as your search will be entirely subject to these specifications. Focus on what's in the JD.
- *Measurable*: Measure your talent acquisition by collecting and interpreting data such as the amount of time taken to fill a position and the position's retention rate. There are many key performance indicators (KPIs), measures, models, and formulas you might apply to measure your talent acquisition, some of which will be addressed in the following chapter. These measurements allow you to enhance your future hiring decisions.
- *Aligned*: Align your recruitment strategy with the company's overall goals and objectives. Chapter 3 contains examples and cases you can use to align your recruitment practices with the company's vision.
- *Realistic*: Be realistic, and hire the person you can afford. Match talent profiles with JDs, and don't hire overqualified candidates. Your ultimate goal is to acquire the best fit. The last thing you want to hear is that your turnover rate is high.
- *Time-framed*: Fill positions according to the scheduled plan, and deliver on time. This will reflect positively on your reputation, performance appraisal, and departmental targets.

The Worst Mistakes Recruiters Make during Interviews

Some interview biases might appear throughout the interviewing process. A talent acquisition manager might unintentionally make several major mistakes that hinder recruitment decisions. Bogardus (2009) describes most of the following mistakes in *PHR/SPHR*:

- *Average rating*: This takes place when a recruitment manager can't make a decision on an interview assessment rating scale. Particularly, it occurs when a recruiter is not able to rate a candidate high or low in most factors of an interview assessment form. Perhaps the recruiter prefers to be neutral. In this case, the assessment form does not show strengthens and weaknesses, and the recruitment manager can't make a final decision effectively.

- *Contrast*: This occurs when you compare candidates to one another or to particular individuals. Comparing is not always perfect and might mislead you. You might evaluate a candidate as very good not because he or she is that good, but because of comparison to incompetent or low-profile candidates. You might assume the candidates you found are the only talents available in the market, and you will most likely not search for other talents or even reframe the search to come up with a better short list of talents.

- *Cultural noise*: This takes place when a candidate answers based on what a recruiter desires to hear. So, don't fall on your face!

- *Stereotyping*: This bias occurs because of false assumptions made about people who belong to specific groups. For example, don't assume that a female will not be able to hold a security role or perform a job where she will be lifting heavy weights.

- *Recent candidate*: This takes place when you remember only the most recent candidate. You tend to forget the candidates you met earlier, and the last becomes the best.

- *First impression*: This occurs when you are reluctant to change your first impression. If a candidate is well-spoken at the beginning of the interview and demonstrates excellent communication skills, a bias can occur. You might not change your evaluation—even if that candidate turns out to demonstrate below-average scores on the remaining factors. Conversely, a candidate who behaves badly at the beginning of an interview might be dropped immediately. Even if the candidate shows a better fit based on answers provided for the rest of the interview, the impression has already been made.

- *Gut feeling*: A recruiter relies on the feelings the candidate is engendering or not—regardless of that candidate's qualifications or competencies.

- *Similar to me*: This bias occurs when a candidate shares mutual interests with the recruiter. Maybe you are both big fans of the Lakers. Maybe you both graduated from the same school. Regardless, a recruiter might overlook a candidate's weaknesses because of those shared interests.

- *Leniency:* This is when a recruiter has an easygoing style. It occurs when you make it easy on candidates and rate all of them highly.

- *Horn and halo effects:* The horn effect occurs when a recruiter evaluates a candidate negatively based on a single competency, without paying attention to the other areas of the assessment. The recruiter thinks one negative competency is enough to color the candidate's overall assessment. The halo effect acts in the opposite way, giving the candidate an overall positive assessment based on a single characteristic. These incomplete assessments overlook some main points in a candidate's assessment.

- *Inconsistency:* This is when a recruiter asks different questions to different candidates. A recruiter will eventually have to ask different questions based on each particular scenario, but there should be common ground and initial structure to inform the assessment's main questions.

CHAPTER 2

RECRUITMENT EFFECTIVENESS: MEASURES, MODELS, AND TECHNIQUES

Executive leadership and top management are all asking for data-based decisions. This chapter enlightens you on how to analyze, report, and use hiring measures to improve your talent acquisition. With all proven recruitment techniques, recruiters and human resources (HR) professionals will be able to make the right hiring decisions.

The Recruitment of Excellence (ROE)

Setting key performance indicators (KPIs) and talent acquisition measures might not be as simple as it seems. You need to look comprehensively at many aspects when evaluating your recruitment practices. There are many widely used formulas in the recruitment field, such as time to hire, time to offer, and so on. However, people tend to forget an essential part, which is that time is not the only measurement to consider. It's not the only accurate indicator of how good your recruitment function is. I personally recommend tracking recruitment progress at any point in time by examining the number of vacant versus filled positions. Usually this formula gives you an indication of how your talent acquisition team is progressing over the year. It gives insights into how many positions are filled and how many are still vacant. Let's examine one example to practice.

Calculation Example—Try It

Company XYZ plans to hire twenty positions during 2016: five positions in IT, ten positions in finance, and five positions in the audit department. In October 2016, before the year's end, the recruitment progress is that five positions have been filled in IT and seven positions have been filled in finance.

Solution

The number of filled positions (twelve) divided by the number of requested positions (twenty) equals 60 percent. What that percentage means is that 60 percent of positions requested for the year have been filled and 40 percent of positions remain vacant. A perfect outcome would be hiring all twenty positions and fulfilling the man-power recruitment plan for 2016. This formula is effective for examining how far or close you are from hitting your hiring target.

Recruitment Evaluation

I have discussed a general rule to determine how well a recruiter is doing over the year in terms of positions filled and positions vacant. However, I have not focused yet on how excellent your hiring is. The lists of KPIs companies set for recruitment is long, but most formulas are used without paying attention to the fact that a recruiter is not the only player in this game. Department heads who are filling out job requisitions and demanding additional staff may also delay hiring due to their busy schedules and perhaps lack of effective communication with the recruitment department regarding hiring. There are also periodic variations in labor regulations that impact the performance of recruitment practices. Last, struggling companies sometimes put hiring on hold to align recruitment strategies with financial performance, and this can lead to fluctuating recruitment productivity.

The message that has to be spread is that putting emphasis solely on time might destructively influence the quality of your recruits. I recommend shifting the focus away from timing factors and use a comprehensive talent acquisition framework such as the recruitment of excellence.

The Recruitment of Excellence (ROE) Framework: Time, Quality, and Retention

The ROE framework focuses on the main elements that talent acquisition managers, HR professionals, and HR department heads can incorporate to have comprehensive evaluations of the year's new hires (see figure 2.1).

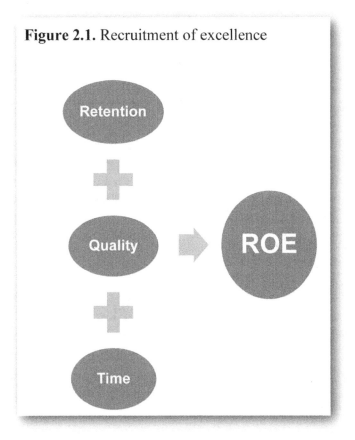

Figure 2.1. Recruitment of excellence

The ROE involves evaluating the excellence of recruits based on three vital fundamentals—retention, quality, and time. These measure the success of your talent acquisition.

To explain retention, quality, and time fundamentals, I will describe the formula for each and provide practical insight into how to implement the ROE framework:

- *Time to hire*: (Total number of positions filled on time ÷ Total number of requested positions filled)
  Divide the total number of positions that were filled on time by the total number of requested positions filled.
  Note that this time frame is defined according to the company's hiring standards. It could be thirty or sixty days.
- *Quality of hire*: (Total number of new hires who received a satisfactory performance rating ÷ Total number of requested positions filled)
  Divide the total number of new hires who received a satisfactory performance rating by the total number of requested positions filled.
  Note that a satisfactory performance rating could be four out of five on a performance appraisal. This is also defined by the company's standards.
- *Retention*: (Total number of new hires who successfully completed a period of time ÷ Total number of requested positions filled)
  Divide the total number of new hires who successfully completed a period of time by the total number of requested positions filled.
  Note that the company's standards can define "period of time." For example, it could be a probationary period of three months or completion of one year of service.

Weight of Recruitment of Excellence Elements

Time, quality, and retention are all fundamentals of the ROE framework. However, recruiters have to allocate different weights to each element of the framework. This depends on your company's view on each element's importance and impact. You might allocate the weights below to each element:

- Time to hire receives 30 percent.
- Quality of hire receives 30 percent.
- Retention receives 40 percent.

The following is an in-depth example where all fundamentals (time, quality, and retention) are incorporated into the ROE framework.

Calculation Example—Try It

Assume a recruiter has been tasked with filling twelve positions for 2016 for company ZY. It's a common standard within the company to fill positions within two months (sixty days). Also, the probation evaluation of a new hire has to be executed upon completion of three months of service. The recruiter has to collect all performance appraisals of the new hires at the end of the year. Company ZY has a performance appraisal scale where four is excellent, three is above expectations, two is meets expectations, and one is below expectations. However, company ZY considers high performers those who achieve three or above. The overall status of time to hire, quality of hire, and retention is shown in table 2.1. Weights are allocated in the table as follows: time is 30 percent, quality is 30 percent, and retention is 40 percent.

Table 2.1.

Recruitment of excellence	Observations
Time to hire	Nine filled on time (within sixty days), one filled late, two vacant
Quality of hire	Six achieved three or above on performance scales
Retention	Eight successfully completed probationary period

What is the ROE percentage in this case?

Solution

ROE = time to hire + quality of hire + retention. In this example, that's $(9 \div 10) + (6 \div 10) + (8 \div 10)$. Note that the number of positions filled is ten.

ROE = 0.9 + 0.6 + 0.8. (That's 90 percent + 60 percent + 80 percent.) Remember, the weights are 30 percent, 30 percent, and 40 percent.

ROE = $(90 \times 30 \div 100) + (60 \times 30 \div 100) + (80 \times 40 \div 100) = 27 + 18 + 32 = 77$.

The ROE is 77 percent. Based on the three weighted fundamentals (time to hire, quality of hire, and retention), the overall percentage of excellence is 77 percent.

Evaluation of Recruitment Channels

You will have to deeply analyze your recruitment channels to gain a comprehensive view of how candidates are applying to your jobs and which gates they are applying through. How effective are your channels? Which ones need improvement? Explore how many candidates have been hired through newspapers, the company's website, and so on. Which channels are used effectively, and which ones are not?

In general, sources such as the company's website, newspapers, job portals, social media sites, referrals, and executive-search firms are considered the main channels of recruitment and talent acquisition. One critical question can be incorporated into your analysis of recruitment sources: How did you hear about us?

Below is an example of one such analysis. It is used to measure the number of résumés or profiles you are receiving through the career website each month during the year.

Figure 2.2.

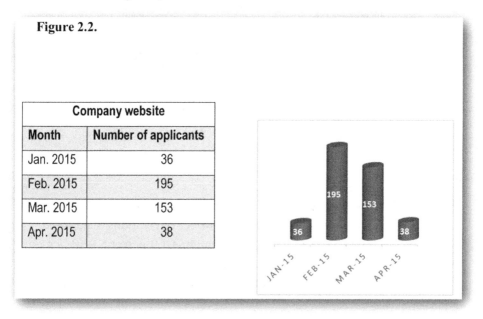

Company website	
Month	Number of applicants
Jan. 2015	36
Feb. 2015	195
Mar. 2015	153
Apr. 2015	38

Figure 2.2 shows there was a rich pool of candidates during February and March. Numerous applicants applied through the career website during that time. In January and April, however, hiring was considered

slow. Perhaps the company was not doing well advertising posts during these months.

Through analyzing your company's career website in relation to the number of applicants, you will be able to recognize when you have a slow hiring season. It will also show what months or periods you can expect a large number of applicants to use your career website.

Similarly, this approach can also be used to measure the impact of job posts on the career website. Posting jobs on LinkedIn or in newspapers will positively influence your career website. Remember, if you post a job ad in a newspaper, you should measure the traffic on your career website after that post is announced.

To get a broader perspective, if you hired all positions (according to the man-power plan), you might consider making a list of all positions along with their hiring sources. This will provide a comprehensive view of how effective your recruitment channels are and which sources of hiring require further development. Figure 2.3 illustrates all hires in 2015 and their associated sources.

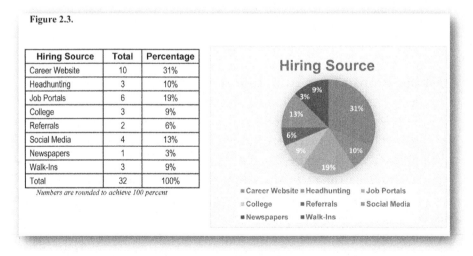

Figure 2.3.

Hiring Source	Total	Percentage
Career Website	10	31%
Headhunting	3	10%
Job Portals	6	19%
College	3	9%
Referrals	2	6%
Social Media	4	13%
Newspapers	1	3%
Walk-Ins	3	9%
Total	32	100%

Numbers are rounded to achieve 100 percent

Figure 2.3 shows thirty-two total hires for the year. The most effective source is the career website, and the second most effective source is job portals. On the other hand, the company needs to enhance the newspaper source. It represents only 3 percent of total hires.

Selection Ratio

Do you have a good number of applicants to hire? *Selection ratio* shows the relationship between job positions and the number of applicants. It basically answers whether you have many qualified candidates to select from or have limited options. To calculate this, divide the number of positions by the number of qualified applicants (Caruth and Handlogten 1997).

The lower the ratio, the better options (qualified candidates) you have to select from. A ratio closer to zero indicates there are many qualified candidates for your positions. Let's examine two examples to demonstrate:

1. You have two vacant positions in auditing, and you have three qualified candidates applying for these two roles. The selection ratio will be 2 ÷ 3 = 0.6.
2. You have two vacant positions in auditing, and you have ten qualified candidates applying for these two roles. The selection ratio will be 2 ÷ 10 = 0.2. That is a better ratio than in the first example. It indicates there are many candidates to consider for the two positions in auditing.

Dashboard: Monitor Your Talent Acquisition Practices

Over the year, you need to monitor the progress of your recruitment function and how this vital function has been delivering. I recommend focusing on core tasks, competencies defined for the recruitment function, and developmental areas. Figure 2.4 is a dashboard. It's based on the general evaluation of departmental tasks, competencies, and areas of development. The main purpose behind such a dashboard is following up, tracking, and overseeing recruitment performance.

You will have to evaluate how your team achieves in relation to each task. This will give you room to follow up on tasks, overcome obstacles, or enhance the recruitment process over the year.

You might appraise monthly, quarterly, or as your business needs, but the bottom line is that you have to monitor the progress of your recruitment over the year. Don't wait until the performance review deadline. A solid dashboard will allow you to overcome challenges your talent acquisition team might face.

Recruitment Department

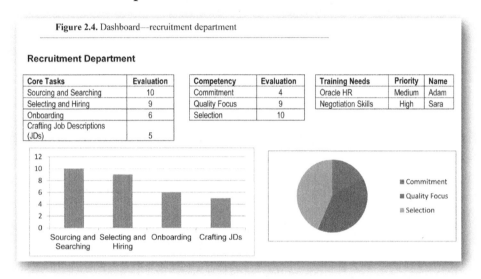

Figure 2.4. Dashboard—recruitment department

Recruitment Department

Core Tasks	Evaluation
Sourcing and Searching	10
Selecting and Hiring	9
Onboarding	6
Crafting Job Descriptions (JDs)	5

Competency	Evaluation
Commitment	4
Quality Focus	9
Selection	10

Training Needs	Priority	Name
Oracle HR	Medium	Adam
Negotiation Skills	High	Sara

As figure 2.4 shows, the company selected three main competencies for the recruitment function. They are commitment, quality focus, and selection. These are overall departmental (functional) competencies that all hiring staffs should acquire. This team mastered the selection competency but did not meet expectations on commitment.

Similarly, you can do evaluation on another essential element—the core tasks of the recruiting department. These tasks are sourcing and searching, selecting and hiring, onboarding, and crafting job descriptions (JDs). As shown in figure 2.4, all scores are out of ten. Recruitment scored a perfect ten in the sources and searching category, but it needed to improve on crafting JDs. The score for this task was low.

Finally, the area of improvement is an imperative element of your dashboard. This is where you have to focus on the knowledge and skills development of staff in the hiring department. Therefore, as seen in figure 2.4, it is high priority to assign Sara to attend negotiation-skills training as part of her soft-skills development.

The Career Levels of Talents

Conducting analysis to identify the number of talents within the company might not be enough. Examining how many are at each different level is imperative to identifying any shortage of talents across career levels. You might have a large number of talents, but those talents might all be occupying junior positions. Therefore, how will your company perform at its best?

I recommend mapping your talents across the company (see table 2.2). Analyze where your talents are placed based on your organizational structures, grades, and career levels.

Table 2.2.

Level	Top-notch talents
Top management	3
Senior management	4
Middle management	2
Professional staff	7
Labor	4
Note: The total number of staff is fifty employees.	

The table indicates only 8 percent of talents are at the labor level (four out of fifty). Therefore, this is a group to focus on during future hiring efforts and perhaps a place to develop existing members. On the other hand, the same table shows 14 percent of talents are at the professional staff level (seven out of fifty). Maintaining a high percentage in each category is critical for successful business achievements.

The overall talent across the whole company is 40 percent. This is calculated by dividing the total number of talents by the total number of staff.

Your talents are identified based on how your company views talents. (This was further explained in chapter 1.) You might view your talents as high performers, subject matter experts, highly competent employees, and so on.

Calculation Example—Try It

Assume your company's size is one hundred employees, and the definition of talent within your company is anyone who scores five out of five on a performance scale, where five means a person significantly exceeds performance expectations. After appraising all employees, thirty scored five out of five. What is the talent percentage?

Solution

The talent percentage is $30 \div 100 = 0.3$. That's 30 percent.

Talents' Salaries

Recruiters have to expand their knowledge of and maximize their exposure to compensation and benefit practices. In particular, this means salary surveys and benchmark administration. The decision of setting a salary package or establishing certain pay might not be yours, and there might be other compensation and benefit professionals who specialize in this area. However, you will have to review competitors' pay and develop your strategy based on what they are offering. You might play a strategic role through hiring top-notch talents without exceeding budget allocated to a vacant position. However, you will not be able to hire top-notch talents if you do not pay well. Even if you do, they will soon leave.

Benchmarking salaries is essential before you start your top-notch hiring. As I learned from Hay Group (2013), you should select a sample to compare your data (salaries) to. Also, you will have to decide on the comparison factor. Is it size, nationality, industry, or another factor? Your company might view industry as the most relevant criterion. Others might believe it is the size of the organization. You can also combine both industry and size, but whatever factors you select, make sure to get accurate comparisons.

Within the benchmarking frame, the decision to exceed market value or perhaps match average salaries is all based on the company's strategy. Some companies aim to match within the twenty-fifth percentile. That's where 75 percent of market data is above this point, and 25 percent is below.

On the other hand, some companies aim to match within the seventy-fifth percentile of the market. That means 25 percent of market data is above this point, and 75 percent is below.

Generally speaking, the best benchmarking plan, at least from my view, is to match the median of the market. That means 50 percent of market data is above this point, and 50 percent is below (see table 2.3).

The bottom line is that it is an effective approach to be fully aware of where your salaries stand in comparison to the market. That way, you can plan your talent acquisition strategy accordingly.

In terms of strategy (based on results of your benchmarking), if the salary you offer is below market value, emphasize nonmonetary incentives, such as having the best working environment or offering training and development to staff. Conversely, if your offer is above market value, then seal deals by showing how much more you are investing to acquire talents.

Negotiations to fill positions are not as easy as they seem. After a long process, the last thing you want to hear is that the offer has been turned down. Because of this, benchmark your salaries with competitors and set up a strategy for talent acquisition.

Table 2.3.

Position	Company's salary	Median salary across all market	Median salary of top ten companies in market	Median of competitors based on industry
IT security officer	$10,000	$11,500	$12,000	$9,800
HR manager	$15,000	$16,000	$16,000	$17,000
Secretary	$4,000	$3,700	$4,000	$4,200

Note: Numbers are for illustrative purposes only and do not reflect actual salaries.

I highly suggest doing the following:

- List all positions requested to be filled.
- Benchmark salaries based on size, industry, or another feasible factor.
- Align your recruitment strategy with the salary you can offer.
- Hire based on your findings.

Applying SWOT to Talent Acquisition

We are all familiar with the popular SWOT strategic instrument, which is an acronym for Strengths, Weaknesses, Opportunities, and Threats. SWOT, which was also explained in Bogardus's (2009) PHR/SPHR study guide, is utilized to evaluate internal factors: Strengths and Weaknesses, as well as external factors in the shape of Opportunities and Threats.

This strategic instrument has been widely used by top management in helping to achieve a company's goals and vision. Therefore, recruiters and talent acquisition managers should apply this instrument to connect with the company's vision and strategy.

The focus will definitely be on people in the sense of how can you strengthen your company with talents, improve on your talent acquisition, and scan the market comprehensively from a workforce planning perspective.

Before explaining the arms of SWOT—Strengths, Weaknesses, Opportunities, and Threats—and showing their connection with your recruitment practice, I suggest following two steps. These two steps will guide you in effectively using the recruitment SWOT analysis:

1) When measuring internal factors, Strengths and Weaknesses, your main objective is to evaluate your company against your competitors. You will consider the following:
   Where does your company stand against the market? Where are you better and where are you weak(er)? What is your distinguishing advantage?

2) When measuring external factors, Opportunities and Threats, your main objective is to scan the market and consider the following: **What are the risks and how to take full advantages of opportunities?**

Below is a list of some fundamental factors to consider upon evaluating your SWOT:

- talents, meaning availability of talents, high performers, and senior leaders
- company, in terms of image, location, brand, reputation, and ranking
- financial resources, and benefits and salaries of employees
- internal hiring process
- economic, political, legal, or technological factors

Strengths and Weaknesses

The question you should be considering at this stage is where does your company stand against the market? You are evaluating whether you have a competitive advantage and does your company perform better than your competitors. You are asking questions to determine what gives you an advantage over other competitors as well as identifying weaknesses, which you will be eliminating to gain competitive advantage. You should be focusing on recruitment by:

- assessing your workforce by determining the number of talents within your company;
- evaluating capabilities of your staff in comparison with your competitors and determining which area(s) in your business lack(s) talents;
- examining your employees' salaries and benefits against the market (*Are you paying your talents higher than competitors? What benefits are you not providing, whereas others do?*);
- evaluating your company location, image, reputation, or brand (*Where do you stand against the market in any type of ranking systems*

such as Employer of Choice, or best working environment to work at?); and

- assessing your hiring process against your competitors (*How good are your job advertisements, and how often do you use social media to attract talents?*).

Opportunity and Threats

In this area, you should consider what risks are on the horizon and how to take an advantage from any opportunity. As you will be dealing with uncontrollable factors, you should be scanning the market carefully to ensure that you are aware of all attractive opportunities or threats that might hinder your business. Again, with your focus on recruitment, you should be considering the following:

- How is the economy affecting your business, and what will be the impact of a high inflation rate on your salaries? Are you going to alter your pay policy? If so, you may have to alter your recruitment strategy accordingly.
- How can you take full advantage of advance technologies? Are you planning to implement the state-of-the-art e-recruitment system to enhance your recruitment process?
- How will labor regulations reflect on your recruitment practice?
- What is the impact of an international company entry on your recruitment? Are you going to be acquiring fewer talents?
- How can new business trends impact on your recruitment?

Recruitment SWOT Example

For illustration purpose, the example below shows strengths, weaknesses, opportunities, and threats of a company that provides IT solutions to its customers. The example is demonstrated from a recruitment angle in order to enhance your strategic thinking in recruitment and talent acquisition.

Strengths:

- availability of top talents in network engineering department
- high pay for employees (first-tier pay)
- low staff-turnover rate
- medical insurance coverage (this is very attractive)

Weaknesses:

- lack of talents in programming department, specifically " programmers"
- ranked very low in "best working environment" survey
- location of company far and out of the city
- no automated recruitment system in place
- lack of talents in supervisory level across the company

Opportunities:

- Acquire talents from company XY, as the company is struggling and facing high staff turnover.
- Apply an e-recruitment system to enhance recruitment process.
- Hire fresh graduates majoring in "software engineering" as there are many batches of graduates at this time compared to last year.

Threats:

- negative feedback on social media
- new employment regulations
- resignation of senior leaders in critical departments to join competitors
- downturn in economy

Recruitment Audit

I suggest examining the compliance level of your recruitment and talent acquisition practices to ensure having a solid recruitment practice within your company. This includes compliance with internal recruitment procedures as well as labor regulations. Investigate past recruitment actions to enhance the quality of future recruitment. This step is best done just prior to entering a new year. That way, you can adjust and correct unsatisfactory actions before it's too late.

The objective of recruitment auditing is not to evaluate overall recruitment practices. After all, every company has its own recruitment practices, and these are based on resources, capacity, and recruitment objectives. However, I aim to audit methods, tactics, and techniques that have been used during the year. This enhances quality and ensures compliance with procedures the following year. Therefore, I suggest examining how you recruit all new hires. To do that, I suggest going through three fundamental steps.

Sampling

You want to investigate how you hired your talents and whether you hired within the time allotted. Who is your sample group to audit? You will also have to examine your compliance level with recruitment policies and procedures.

You have two options: either you can cover all the new recruits (if the number is small), or you can select some files to audit and examine (if time and work duties constrain you). Also, pay attention to diversification. Selecting files to audit from different departments and with different levels of seniority, different ages, and different genders is imperative to reach success.

Auditing

After selecting your sample, you should prepare to ask proper questions to examine compliance and consistency. There are several approaches, including asking open-ended questions, conducting interviews, and administering questionnaires. Regardless of whatever method you choose, use questions that ask about how you hired talents last year, some major mistakes to avoid in the future, and how you can enhance hiring and talent acquisition. Here are some critical points to pay attention to:

- whether employment documents were completed per the company's internal policies and procedures
- whether reference checks and exit interviews were conducted properly
- whether orientation was given the right amount of attention and time
- whether consultancy agreements and executive search contracts were selected effectively
- whether employment offers and contracts were standardized, and whether all internal approvals were obtained
- whether successful implementation of the five *S* method of the recruitment occurred
- whether the time taken to fill positions is in accordance with service-level agreements within the company

Reporting

The objective of the reporting stage is to correct issues and improve for the future. Let that message be clear. You are about to identify weaknesses in compliance as well as risks associated with the lack of compliance or commitment to the recruitment process. All findings, concerns, and observations will be revealed, and an action plan has to be set to develop weak areas in relation to the company's internal standards. (See table 2.4.)

Table 2.4.

Action	2016			
	June	July	Aug.	Sept.
Create job descriptions for all positions	X	X		
Update employment contracts	X			
Complete employment documents of new hires	X	X	X	X

Let's explore table 2.4. If employment contracts are not drafted per labor regulations, an action of updating employment contracts has to be set within a month to avoid any legal disputes. (In this table, that month is June.)

"Complete employment documents of new hires" is another action. This needs to be resolved in four months. (In this table, that's June to September.)

It is essential to report all concerns and set up a correction plan to avoid falling into the same mistakes the following year. The ultimate objective is to set an action plan for each finding, and resolve what is missing or incomplete. An ideal audit report identifies findings and risks and creates an action plan to enhance recruitment and talent acquisition practices.

Satisfaction Levels with Recruitment Practices

Collecting data and receiving feedback from concerned individuals, such as managers or department heads, will definitely assist you in evaluating your performance over the year. At the end of the year, recruiters often plan immediately for the following year. They start hiring again for new positions, but unfortunately, they don't gather feedback from departments about what has been done in relation to recruitment over the year.

Sending questionnaires to all concerned managers in relation to new hires can give you an overview of what has been done correctly or wrongly. This will assist in your next hires—if the proper questions are addressed. The aim of administering questionnaires is to develop and enhance your recruitment practice for the following year and avoid errors you had. The message has to be clear to develop and learn from experience. Table 2.5 shows an example of a survey that can be used to measure your performance for all positions assigned to you.

As usual, you will have to consider the fundamentals of administering questionnaires. This includes proper time of administration, sample selection, and other critical factors that might impact your data collection.

Table 2.5. Example of a survey

Talent acquisition satisfaction survey
Purpose of the survey
The purpose of this recruitment satisfaction survey is to help us serve your recruitment needs more effectively. By understanding where we are meeting expectations, exceeding expectations, or needing to improve, we can allocate our resources to provide better future hiring. So, please provide constructive feedback that we can incorporate into our strategy.
Guidelines
Please circle the response that best represents your view, with 5 being "exceeds expectations" and 1 being "unacceptable." Please select N/A for any questions you don't have enough experience to comment on.
Recruitment staff professionalism:
5   4   3   2   1   N/A
Ability to understand job requirements/job descriptions:
5   4   3   2   1   N/A
Expertise of recruitment staff:
5   4   3   2   1   N/A
Delivery on time:
5   4   3   2   1   N/A
Quality of résumés/CVs provided:
5   4   3   2   1   N/A
Overall performance:
5   4   3   2   1   N/A

Lately, I have noticed several companies investing heavily in designing satisfaction or engagement surveys. However, few have gathered constructive feedback on talent acquisition practices. Surveys provide insightful qualitative data that you might consider along with the quantitative metrics and formulas explained in the beginning of the chapter.

CHAPTER 3

Planning for Top-Notch Hiring: Workforce Planning

M an-power planning is one of the fundamental elements of talent acquisition. Your hiring will entirely depend on what you plan for. Thus, in this chapter, I will point out main frameworks and formulas that will assist in your workforce planning. Also, chapter 3 describes the nationalization concept and shows the importance of aligning the talent acquisition plan with your company's strategic goals.

Alignment of Recruitment Strategies and the Company's Goals and Objectives

You will have to align your talent acquisition plan with the company's strategic goals. An effective talent acquisition strategy has to be connected to the company's vision and mission.

The following are some examples of common company objectives and how talent acquisition should align accordingly:

1) The first strategic goal is to maximize profit. The goal might be to increase the company's profit by $100 million or to gain a higher market share. These are the most common types of goals. After all, why does a company exist? Because of profit.

To align with an objective to maximize profits, recruitment should comply with the allocated company budget. Hire talents per the budgeted plan, and incur no additional costs to attract those talents. This might be difficult in a competitive market, but this is how effective recruitment plays a role in reducing cost and increasing profit. Hiring talents based on determined salaries and negotiating to convince talents to join your company are proof of your contribution to the company's bottom line.

2) The second strategic goal is to increase brand awareness or change customer perception. The recruitment strategy is to lead a campaign to be on the list of the top one hundred companies with the best working environments and to focus on becoming an employer of choice. Build a referral recruitment system, enhance your social media presence, and expand your subscriptions in social media websites, such as LinkedIn and other job portals. Advertising your jobs everywhere will impact your overall objective. Work with your marketing team to create an attractive career website. Critical positions that have a direct impact on your bottom line, such as marketing specialists, should be your first priority to fill with top-notch talents.

3) The third strategic goal is to lead the market through technological innovation. The recruitment strategy is to increase hiring efficiency by having a solid online recruitment process in place. Speed and less paperwork should be embedded in that process. Enhance the technology of recruitment, and align with technological recruitment trends. Your hiring objective will be to approach IT professionals, research and development (R and D) managers, and other critical positions.

4) The fourth strategic goal is to enter a new market. The recruitment strategy is to diversify your workforce and focus on hiring from nationalities and cultures of markets you aim to enter. Emphasize language, multiculturalism, and communication as core competencies to assess at the time of hiring. Incorporate multicultural assessments as part of your selection approach. Finally, understand the new market's labor regulations in relation to recruitment and talent acquisition.

5) The fifth strategic goal is growth and expansion. Massive recruitment is the key. Focus on how long it takes to fill key positions along

with quality in hiring. Quick hiring will definitely require an online recruitment tool to smooth the process and increase efficiency.

Critical Positions

Critical positions are those that have direct as well as positive impact on the company's bottom line. The talent acquisition team will have to craft recruitment strategies to connect with the company's vision and mission. What positions are most critical to your company's vision?

You will have to be very careful if you plan to communicate your view of critical versus noncritical positions. All employees view their positions as essential, and no one wants his or her position classified as noncritical. All positions will impact your business—directly or indirectly. You don't want to hurt feelings by distinguishing between critical and noncritical roles, but top management might favor some roles due to their direct impact on business strategy. Therefore, depending on the business's, industry's, or company's short- or long-term objectives, a recruiter will have to identify critical roles and prioritize hiring these roles accordingly.

- If a company's objective is to maximize profit and increase sales, the recruiter might focus on critical positions such as sales and collection managers, who increase profits. Other roles will definitely impact the process, but they will not match the contributions of sales or collection managers.
- If a company's objective is the development of new products, recruitment might focus on critical positions such as the R and D director, the distribution manager, or the marketing head. These people play essential roles in marketing new products in the industry.
- If a company's objective is to have the best working environment, recruitment might aim to attract strategic HR professionals or corporate communication managers. They can work together to create an attractive environment.
- If a company's aim is to lead through technological innovation, recruitment should definitely look at IT professionals. They will add value and support your mission.

- If a start-up's aim is to manufacture plastics and gain a huge market share, recruitment might focus on production, warehouse, and distribution directors. These people have the capabilities to build effective manufacturing systems. (See figure 3.1.)

This approach of mapping all positions in terms of criticality is a vital planning technique—even if it is done through reasonable assumptions. Mapping critical positions assists your plan for hiring. Which position should you start sourcing for first? Which one should you prioritize? Which one should you advertise more widely?

You will be capable of answering all these questions when you sit down with the top management team and map critical positions from the highest priority to the lowest.

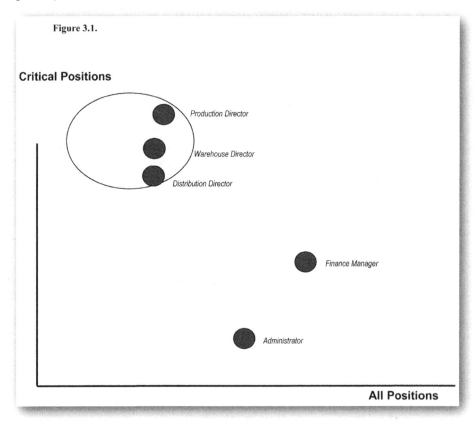

Figure 3.1.

Critical Positions

Production Director

Warehouse Director

Distribution Director

Finance Manager

Administrator

All Positions

Considering which positions are most difficult to fill will let you pay more attention to these roles and place you on the right track to fill positions according to the planned schedule. However, in many cases, a position might be difficult to fill in your industry but not in others. Also, each market is different—a position might be difficult to fill in the Middle East, but it might not be difficult in the United States or Europe.

You can always refer to historical hiring data to have an idea of positions that took a lot of time to fill. Meeting with subject matter experts in each department might reveal past struggles or challenges encountered upon filling vacant positions.

The approach of identifying critical positions will guide you in planning your hiring and broaden your knowledge. This will help you decide which positions to focus on and how to plan for these positions differently. It will also help you learn from past experiences. You can plan to allocate more resources to these positions to avoid late delivery with hiring. For example, assign two recruiters to work on one difficult position. You could also invest more in job advertisements and marketing.

Definition of a Hard-to-Fill Position

So, how do you determine a position is difficult? There are some factors to consider in defining a difficult role:

- If a position requires unique skills or specific capabilities, this role is difficult to fill.
- When your pool of candidates in your industry is too small, then you have a shortage of people for specific professions. For example, assume there aren't too many insurance managers in your market. This is because the insurance industry is still growing in this specific market, and only a couple of insurance companies exist. However, this might not be the case in other markets such as the United States. In that country, there are many insurance companies in each state.
- Highly paid positions will always be difficult due to budget constraints. You have to figure out how you will attract talented candidates without paying what they are expecting.

- Senior roles are hard to fill because these people are not actively looking for change. In general, these workers might not move easily due to higher commitments, responsibilities, and levels of involvement in projects. You will need to double your effort to convince these workers to leave their current senior roles. Many are passive candidates. Perhaps their first preference is to be approached through headhunters and executive-search firms.

Mapping Hard-to-Fill Positions

I recommend you map all positions based on their hiring difficulty as this assists you in your workforce planning. If you don't have many graduates holding degrees and professional certifications in IT security, then perhaps the IT security officer will be a hard-to-fill position. Or the chief transformation officer is a senior position that requires unique transformational skills and may be hard to fill. Again, mapping hard-to-fill positions depends on the market and industry and your view toward difficulty in hiring of some positions.

Workforce Planning: Fundamental Elements of Talent Acquisition

Workforce planning is one of the fundamental elements of recruitment and talent acquisition. Your hiring will entirely depend on what you plan for. Thus, I will point out main points, frameworks, and formulas that will assist in your workforce forecasting and planning. The question is how many employees you need to fulfill the company's needs.

Caruth and Handlogten (1997, 122) define HR planning as "a systematic, ongoing activity that ensures that an organization has the right number and kind of people in the right jobs at the right time so that the institution can achieve its stated objectives." You don't want to determine the wrong number of employees and then require those people to achieve your company's goals. Shortage of staff will impact your productivity and might foster a stressful working environment. Surplus staff, however, increases the company's costs and expenses. You don't want to hire more than you need.

Unfortunately, several companies have unintentionally made both of these mistakes due to poor man-power planning.

Workforce planning will be affected by factors such as labor regulations, political factors, technological innovations, and the company's strategic plans. These plans include entering new markets and experiencing expansion, growth, mergers, and acquisitions. These are all essential drivers for man-power planning.

A piece of advice for man-power planners is to team up with finance managers. Don't forget that a finance manager will play an essential role during the process as such role may approve head counts budget. Thus, finance cooperation will make your process much easier.

Usually, companies conduct their planning at the end of each year, but this depends on the industry and the company's size.

The Number of Leaders Needed

Leaders are the bones of the organization, but you have to analyze the company and decide whether you have the right number of senior talents to lead the company to fulfill its vision and objectives. How many leaders do you need to fulfill a company's objectives? You will have to answer this question to save money from being spent on surplus leaders.

Talent acquisition managers should consider deciding on the required number of leaders based on the company's size in order to plan for an effective workforce planning. Ulrich and Smallwood (n.d.) state that the number of leaders should be the square root of the total number of company employees. Table 3.1 shows examples from companies of different sizes.

Table 3.1.

Total number of employees	Number of leaders
2,500	50
100	10

If an organization has one hundred employees, the square root of one hundred reveals that ten leaders are required. This formula is good for forecasting man power. Refer to it during your man-power and forecasting planning sessions. However, it is definitely not to be entirely relied on. The nature of the business and the market as well as other factors can impact results.

Management's Span of Control: Increase the Efficiency of Your Company

To increase the efficiency and productivity of your company, you should analyze your management's span of control. How many direct reports are reporting to a manager? Using the management's span of control formula will definitely broaden your view in regard to your company's organizational structure, and it will assist you in planning for your future hiring. Based on this analysis, you will contribute to building effective organizational structures within your company. It is essential to look at the cost of the management hierarchy and think about how to reduce that cost while maintaining a high level of efficiency within your management team.

How do you calculate your management's span of control? This calculation is described in the Australian Public Service Commission's (2015) article "Span of Control": the average management span of control can be found by dividing the total number of employees minus one by the total number of managers with direct reports.

Average Span of Control: (Total number of employees − 1) ÷ total number of manager with direct reports

Calculation Example—Try It

An IT department has ten managers with direct reports. The total number of employees of the department is ninety. What is the management's span-of-control ratio of the department?

Solution

You will have to calculate the total number of employees minus one, and then you will have to divide by the total number of managers with direct reports. For this IT department, the numbers will be (90 – 1) ÷ 10 = 8.9. That means the span-of-control ratio is 1:9. That also means that on average, nine employees within the IT department report directly to one manager.

Wanting a wide or narrow span of control depends on an organization's size, culture, and management style. Span of control is essential to understanding what kind of reporting or hierarchy you aim to put in place. Are you aiming to endorse delegation, empowerment, and independence, or do you want to create a centralized reporting system where managers control decisions?

Tom McMullen from Hay Group (2009) showed some models in relation to the span-of-control scope. These were based on the following best practices (see figure 3.2):

- *Common*: In this model, a manager has three to five direct reports. The size enforces management delegation, and the possibility of defining a successor to a manager is high. This model supports empowerment, and it is mostly used.
- *Broad*: This model gives six to ten direct reports to each manager. This model tends to be a centralized one. Succession planning might be difficult to implement.
- *Very large*: This is a centralized model in which there are more than ten direct reports to each manager. Finding a successor is almost impossible.

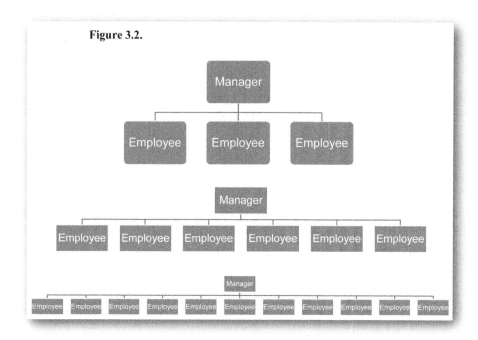

Figure 3.2.

Workforce planners should incorporate the management's span-of-control ratio into man-power planning and forecasting. It gives an indication of how many managers need to be hired to align with the organizational structure and allocated budget.

Another way to map your employees according to the span-of-control element is through the company's different organizational levels—executive directors, senior managers, middle managers, professional staff, and laborers. A matrix adapted from Floros and Khayzaran (2015) appears in table 3.2.

Table 3.2. Number of direct reports

Level	Number of direct reports			
	One to four	Five to seven	Eight to ten	More than ten
Executive Directors	*One Director*	*One Director*		
Senior Management		*One Senior Manager*		
Middle Management	*Two Managers*			
Professional Staff				
Laborers				

To explain the matrix shown in table 3.2:

- There are two executive directors within the company. Of the two, one executive director has one to four direct reports. Five to seven employees report to the second executive director.
- There is one senior manager who has five to seven direct reports.
- There are two middle managers who have one to four direct reports.

Forecasting

You might forecast and make assumptions about the right number of staff you will need. Forecasting comes up with the final estimate of the total number of staff. Forecasting for each department is imperative, but it's based on assumptions and expectations. You might reach the year-end, therefore, with a different total number of staff than the forecasted one.

Caruth and Handlogten (1997) identified many factors to consider when forecasting additional staff. Examples include internal transfers into departments, promotions, new hires, replacement positions, and additional new roles. Factors to consider when forecasting elimination of staff include: terminations, resignations, deaths, retirements, internal transfers out of the department, and the elimination of roles.

The In-and-Out Workforce Planning Model

Which positions will be considered when forecasting and which will be eliminated? Basically, this model's main objective is to address this critical question. Liaise with the department heads before the year-end to know which positions will be included the following year and which will not. This is the fundamental idea of the in-and-out model.

The focus of the in-and-out model is on positions, not incumbents. This model consists of four stages that have to be executed for each department.

Stage One: List Current Approved Positions

List all current positions as of the time you decided to conduct the man-power planning. I suggest doing this at year-end. The list should contain detailed information for each position, such as the incumbent's name, grade, and so on. At this stage, you will be meeting with each department, going through all the positions, and listing the department's approved positions. (This will include vacancies that are approved but haven't been filled during the year.)

Table 3.3 lists all positions for an information technology (IT) department—even the vacant positions. This includes the project manager position, which is grade thirteen, vacant, and has no incumbent. The example in the table assumes the man-power plan was conducted at the end of 2015 to come up with a required head count for the IT department in 2016.

Table 3.3.

IT department			Man-power plan for 2016	
All positions	**Grade**	**Incumbent**	**In/Out**	**Action**
IT Manager	14	Mark		
Programmer	9	John		
Senior Programmer	12	Mohammed		
Secretary	6	Mike		
Designer	11	Jim		
Project Manager	13	X		
Network Manager	12	Jake		
Technician	7	Bill		
Number of Positions at End of 2016				

"X" means the position is vacant.

Stage Two: Decide Which Positions to Include and Not Include

Decide which positions are in and which are out for 2016. Start evaluating your positions (as seen in table 3.4). *In positions* are positions that will be included the following year. And *out positions* are positions that will not be included the following year.

You will have to justify the reasons for including positions or not. Again, you are analyzing positions, not incumbents. If you are thinking about terminating an employee, the position will still be open, but the job holder will be replaced. As another example, if you aim to cancel a position due to budget constraints, then the position is canceled. No job holder will be able to occupy such as role. Those two examples are important to understanding stage three.

Table 3.4.

IT department			Man-power plan for 2016		
All positions	**Grade**	**Incumbent**	**In/Out**		**Action**
IT Manager	14	Mark	In		Continue
Programmer	9	John	In		Continue
Senior Programmer	12	Mohammed	In		Continue
Secretary	6	Mike	In		Continue
Designer	11	Jim	Out		Canceled
Project Manager	13	X	In		Continue
Network Manager	12	Jake	In		Continue
Technician	7	Bill	Out		Canceled
Number of Positions at End of 2016					

"X" means the position is vacant.

Stage Three: List Approved New Positions

Get approval for all new proposed positions. That way, you can add all of them to the man-power plan. You might have to review the department's request for new positions before you consider any. Most companies use position analysis questionnaires (PAQs) to analyze required jobs. PAQs also help determine whether a new position is needed, that role's level (managerial or not), and how many direct reports that role would have—all questions that need to be addressed. The most important part of any PAQ is to do the following:

1. List all primary tasks and main responsibilities.
2. Identify the total annual percentage of time devoted across all listed tasks.
3. Ensure the total percentage of time equals 100 percent.

Approving new positions will naturally add costs and expenses. Therefore, you will have to ensure there is a need for new positions. Challenging your business and validating that these new positions are required to achieve the company's objectives are essential at this point.

Table 3.5.

IT department				Man-power plan for 2016
All positions	Grade	Incumbent	In/Out	Action
IT Manager	14	Mark	In	Continue
Programmer	9	John	In	Continue
Senior Programmer	12	Mohammed	In	Continue
Secretary	6	Mike	In	Continue
Designer	11	Jim	Out	Canceled
Project Manager	13	X	In	Continue
Network Manager	12	Jake	In	Continue
Technician	7	Bill	Out	Canceled
Programmer	9	X	In	Add position to replace technician
Number of Positions at End of 2016				

"X" means the position is vacant.

In table 3.5, the programmer position has been added as a new position for 2016. It is also a replacement of Bill's technician position, but its grade has been increased to match the existing programmer position.

Stage Four: Finalize Your Man-Power Plan

Count all in positions that you will plan to fill in the following year. Table 3.6 shows the final seven approved positions for 2016.

Table 3.6.

IT department				Man-power plan for 2016
All positions	Grade	Incumbent	In/Out	Action
IT Manager	14	Mark	In	Continue
Programmer	9	John	In	Continue
Senior Programmer	12	Mohammed	In	Continue
Secretary	6	Mike	In	Continue
Project Manager	13	X	In	Continue
Network Manager	12	Jake	In	Continue
Programmer	9	X	In	Add position to replace technician
Number of Positions at End of 2016				7

"X" means the position is vacant.

Calculation Example—Try It

A finance department has five employees working within the department. This is described in table 3.7.

Table 3.7.

Finance department			Man-power plan for 2016
All positions	**Grade**	**Incumbent**	
Financial Controller	14	Sara	
Accountant	8	Adam	
Finance Manager	13	X	
Secretary	5	Lila	
Accountant	7	Bill	
Senior Accountant	12	John	
Number of Positions at End of 2016			**6**

"X" means the position is vacant.

Conduct a man-power plan for 2016 based on the in-and-out model. However, first consider the following. It is the end of 2015, and there are six approved positions (per table 3.7). The finance department decided to cancel Bill's position (a grade-seven accountant) after he submitted his resignation. A grade-eleven senior accountant replaces Bill's position. By doing so, the department will end up with two senior accountants. Although the finance manager's position is open, the department decided to transfer it to next year (2016). The finance department decided to terminate Lila. The department will cancel the secretary position as there will be no need for this role anymore.

Solution

Follow the four steps of the in-and-out model:

1. List all current approved positions of 2015. These are financial controller, accountant, finance manager, secretary, accountant, and senior accountant.

2. Decide which positions are in and which are out for 2016. The out positions are the grade-seven accountant and the secretary. The in positions are the financial controller, the grade-eight accountant, the finance manager, and the senior accountant.

3. List new positions the finance department requested. The only new position is the grade-eleven senior accountant (the replacement position for the grade-seven accountant).

4. Finalize the man-power plan (see table 3.8).

Table 3.8.

Finance department				Man-power plan for 2016
All positions	Grade	Incumbent	In/Out	Action
Financial Controller	14	Sara	In	Continue
Accountant	8	Adam	In	Continue
Finance Manager	13	X	In	Continue
Senior Accountant	12	John	In	Continue
Senior Accountant	11	X	In	Add position to replace accountant
Number of Positions at End of 2016	5			

"X" means the position is vacant.

The number of positions has been reduced to five. There are only three employees holding positions within the finance department, and the other positions are approved but vacant.

Nationalization of Jobs

How many nationals are represented in your workforce? How many nationals do you need to acquire? What is your overall nationalization percentage?

In many countries, especially in the Middle East, the concept of nationalization, in which nationals are given opportunities to hold positions with a company, is quite common and required by labor regulations. Therefore, one main objective of talent acquisition is nationalization. You want to hire nationals for the company's vacancies in order to fulfill labor regulations. A shortage of national staff members will have an impact on business because governments in many countries will place restrictions on companies for not fulfilling the required nationalization percentage. These restrictions impact business productivity and overall company objectives.

So, how do you calculate your nationalization percentage? Divide the total number of nationals by the total number of employees.

Calculation Example—Try It

Company XYZ has twenty national employees and forty employees who are not nationals. What is the nationalization percentage of the company?

Divide the total number of nationals by the total number of employees: $20 \div 60 = 0.33$, or 33 percent.

In many countries today, national recruitment has become one of the fundamental goals of recruitment and talent acquisition. Recruitment performance relies (to some degree) on that nationalization percentage being achieved. Thus, I will highlight essential points to assist you in padding your nationalization percentage:

1. Examine labor regulations in relation to national recruitment. What is the national percentage required for your company's size?
2. Ensure buy-in and full support from the top management team to endorse national hiring. A message like this one can be circulated from the top management team:

   It is a great pleasure to share our company's objective of hiring nationals. We totally believe in national talents and aligning with the labor regulation of reaching 30 percent nationalization. The talent acquisition of nationals is one essential objective we aim to fulfill, and we would like you to contribute to our nationalization objective.

   Our success over the last three years has always been due to our acquisition of top-notch talents. This has provided our customers with the best user experience available. To meet the challenges ahead and fulfill our company's expectations, we aim to achieve 30 percent nationalization by hiring highly qualified national talents who can contribute to our vision. We appreciate your ongoing support and belief in national talents, and we look forward to your cooperation with our talent acquisition team.

We wholeheartedly welcome any constructive feedback you might have.

3. Work closely with the department heads to communicate the plan. At this stage, you will have to set nationalization objectives to fulfill (see table 3.9).

Table 3.9.

Department	Nationalization percentage (%)	2017 target percentage (%)
Legal	20	23
Procurement	10	15
HR	40	40
Sales	5	15
Logistics	30	30

Table 3.9 shows that recruitment will have to maintain 40 percent nationalization for the HR department. On the other hand, the sales department has a very low nationalization percentage (5 percent). The target for 2017 is to reach 15 percent by the end of the year.

4. Incorporate your nationalization objectives into your workforce planning. This is critical. You will have to plan for your national positions before you start hiring. This part will entail all types of analyses to assist you in crafting your plan.

   • You will have to explore the market and examine the scarcity of nationals in specific jobs and the availability of nationals at certain career levels (senior management, management, labor positions, and so on). Be realistic. Figure out which positions will have large numbers of applicants and which positions will be difficult to hire nationals for (due to lack of qualifications, lack of expertise, etc.).

- You might identify difficult positions in each department. That way, you can plan to invest more than the allocated budget for positions and advertisements.
- You will have to examine the existing national population within your company. Determine the level at which they are mostly placed (senior management, middle positions, or junior positions). How many national leaders are representing your company?

5. Post jobs and advertisements. Enrich your national talent pool through social media, job portals, and career fairs. Your career website should include attractive sections, such as benefits, testimonials, a cultural explanation, career development options, and so on.
6. Create a friendly working environment to attract national talents to your workplace.
7. Hire top-notch national talents. Basically, this means applying advanced recruitment techniques and effective hiring tactics to find top-notch nationals. Use the man-power plan for guidance.

Depending on cultural and internal norms, there might be resistance to change, or perhaps there might be no preference for nationals. You might, therefore, have to do the following:

- Link the performance of each department to the nationalization percentage achieved. There could be a bonus or variable pay for departments linked to fulfilling the nationalization percentage.
- Train nationals and invest in their development in order to change perspectives and enhance future national hiring.
- Start from the bottom. Hire fresh national graduates. You can develop and build a cost-effective graduate program to attract nationals to join your company.

Nationalization: Development of an Action Plan

The objective of nationalization is to hire required nationals by reinforcing national talent acquisition in order to reach an identified percentage of nationalization by a specific year. Table 3.10 shows an action plan for this purpose.

Table 3.10. Nationalization action plan

Recruitment practice	Delivery time	Owner
Effectively conduct national workforce planning to identify required talents		
Hire top-notch national talents according to national workforce plan		
Emphasize hiring national graduates via advertising at colleges and career fairs		
Exploit social media, job portals, and referral systems to widen the search scope and identify national talent		
Liaise with department heads to ensure the intake of required nationals each year		

Although the scope of this book doesn't include training and professional development, it is essential to show some vital developmental options being incorporated into your nationalization program. Any nationalization program will fail if no attention is paid to the development and career growth of national talents.

Table 3.11 shows practical developmental methods. I adapted these from Ulrich and Smallwood (n.d.). You will need to execute these developmental methods to train your national talents as well as other nonnationals.

Table 3.11.

Development activities	Year one				Year two			
	Q1	Q2	Q3	Q4	Q1	Q2	Q3	Q4
Be responsible for profits and losses								
Conduct 360-degree assessments								
Pursue professional certifications								
Receive coaching and mentoring								
Participate in or lead a special project								
Make a presentation to senior management or the board of directors								
Have exposure to another department								
Take a job assignment in a different company or culture								
Take a training course (at the company, externally, or online)								
Join management committees								
Present at a conference, seminar, or summit								
Read articles, books, or journals								
Expand responsibilities								

CHAPTER 4

ALIGNING COMPETENCIES WITH YOUR RECRUITMENT PRACTICES

The area of competency is popular with recruiters and HR professionals. The final chapter shows how to use relevant competencies in your recruitment practices, and aligning these with your company's strategic objectives. The chapter explains how to use competencies to distinguish between talents and average performers.

Competence Is a Hot Topic These Days

This chapter is all about evaluating competence in recruitment. Competency is an essential part of any competency model used in HR, and it includes training, career development, succession planning, and recruitment. Remember, though, companies view competencies differently. Some name their competencies *functional competencies* for use on the technical side. Some use *behavioral competencies* to measure general behaviors. Others use both functional and behavioral competencies to provide a comprehensive model. The focus in this section is on *general competencies*. These include all types such as technical, core, behavioral, and leadership competencies.

Defining the main competencies required for each role is becoming one of the most common HR practices these days. Doing so allows you to build your job descriptions, performance appraisals, and interview assessment forms based on the competencies you aim to incorporate. The focus in this section will be on interviews and talent acquisition.

Competencies are widely used by recruiters and talent acquisition managers. I encourage most recruiters and human resources (HR) professionals to conduct interviews using guidance from *PHR/SPHR* (Bogardus 2009):

- In *structured interviews*, there are no random questions. You assess your candidate based on planned and organized questions—each candidate receives the same questions in the same order in order to standardize your process. You will definitely probe and ask specific questions based on each case, but some general questions should be standardized.
- In *competency-based job interviews*, you ask specific questions in order to measure how good the candidate is on specific competencies (see table 4.1). Their answers will hopefully be predictive of their future reactions to similar situations. Preferably, a recruiter will identify relevant competencies prior to conducting the interview. Some sample questions include the following:
  - Tell me about a time when you [fill in the competency you want to measure].
  - Describe a situation when you [fill in the competency you want to measure].
  - Give me an example of [fill in the competency you want to measure].

Table 4.1. Competency-based interview assessment form

Competency	Question	Rating		Note
Problem Solving	Tell me about a time when you had to solve a problem within the last year.	❑	Excellent	
		❑	Very good	
		❑	Good	
		❑	Poor	
Teamwork	Describe a situation where others you were working with on a business assignment disagreed with your approaches.	❑	Excellent	
		❑	Very good	
		❑	Good	
		❑	Poor	
Communication	Give me an example of a time when you had to use your presentation skills to influence someone's opinion.	❑	Excellent	
		❑	Very good	
		❑	Good	
		❑	Poor	

Nowadays, candidates are smart enough to appear superb in an interview. This includes, but is not limited to, answering questions the way you want them to be answered. Candidates often search the Internet for the top ten interview questions. They assume you will be asking similar questions. Unfortunately, candidates also give fake answers to show advanced levels of certain competencies related to the job. Therefore, your competencies have to be set to guide you through an effective evaluation and allow you to measure what you intend to evaluate.

As Spencer and Spencer (1993) pointed out in *Competence at Work*, don't jump to conclusions or put your words in the candidate's mouth. Don't even paraphrase what the candidate says. Don't help a candidate. Stay with one subject, be focused, and don't let a candidate jump to different topics. You must evaluate the competencies precisely. If the candidate avoids a line of questioning, ask specific questions to return to the main topic.

I always recommend letting the candidate express what he or she is trying to say. Be an active listener. Think about how you are going to probe.

Table 4.2 shows a list of competencies that might be considered for your company's roles. The focus of this subject is on general competencies rather than classifying competencies into core, behavioral, or technical competencies.

Table 4.2. Competency list

Competency list
Managing change • Teamwork and cooperation • Communication
Strategic thinking • Time management • Project management
Financial planning • Leadership • Empowering others
Operational excellence • Delegation • Decision making
Problem solving • Creativity and innovation • Customer orientation
Attention to details • Developing others • Technical expertise
Analytical thinking • Stress management • Flexibility
Accountability • Dedication and commitment • Planning and organizing
Active listening • Integrity and honesty • Initiative
Emotional intelligence • Project organizing • Conflict management
Managing performance • Managing risks • Entrepreneurship
Interpersonal skills • Coaching and mentoring
Continued learning • Influencing others • Systems thinking

Probing Approach: Explore Further

It's time to explore further, investigate, and ask additional questions. Recruiters tend to probe to gain complete answers or perhaps because they want further details about incidents or projects. Let's be honest—you might not feel the candidate is telling the truth, so you have to probe and probe. You can ask questions such as the following:

- So, are you saying…
- Can you tell me more about…
- So, why did you…

These examples of probing questions will help you gather as much information as possible about how competent your talent is. Remember to take some valuable advice about probing from Spencer and Spencer (1993): Keep your questions short. Use no more than ten words. Probe for facts, and be an investigative reporter. However, don't restrict candidates. Let them express what they want to say.

Simple Language

People tend to confuse themselves and complicate the competency concept by having too many categories—core, behavioral, technical, or leadership competencies. Under each of these categories, there can be up to six sublevels of behavioral indicators or professional levels. Unfortunately, at least from my point of view, the competency-based model has not been successfully implemented yet, and that is due to difficulties we are creating. Why are we making it so difficult? Some major points to highlight within the competency concept include the following:

- Be aware of overlapping competencies due to the nature of the job. Is effective communication a behavioral or a technical competency for a public relations director? People in that position spend most of their days in internal and external communication.
- Validate your competency dictionary definition and proficiency levels. How many opinions on these competency definitions and levels have you collected? How many subject matter experts were involved? How frequently have you validated your dictionary?

Designing a solid competency model will depend on the nature of the business, support from top management, and how other departments cooperate and contribute to the model. The bottom line, however, is to use a simple language that everyone understands.

Competency in Recruitment and Talent Acquisition

How do we use competencies to distinguish between talents and average performers? The process below will guide you to effectively use competencies in recruitment and talent acquisition.

1) Identify all the vacant positions that need to be filled (per an approved man-power plan). In the beginning stage, you have to list all positions required for the year that you will aim to fill.

2) Identify all of the required competencies for each position. You will have to design your competency hiring tool kit (see table 4.2) to do this. You might also distinguish between technical and nontechnical competencies or incorporate all of them in one tool kit.

After identifying the positions to fill and developing your tool kit, you may decide to have no more than four to ten competencies for each position. That's in addition to your company's values, which are competencies, too.

If you are going to list all positions you need to fill and identify associated competencies, you could use table 4.3 as a starting point. I selected four competencies for each position for illustrative purposes.

Table 4.3.

Position	Competencies
Administrative assistant	Typing
	Filing
	Time management
	Scheduling
Financial analyst	Financial planning
	Analytical thinking
	Operational excellence
	Organization
Recruitment manager	Communication
	Negotiation
	Selection skills
	Time management

It is essential to comprehensively define each competency. For example, a definition of "visioning" might be the capacity to develop a new vision for the company and set up future missions and goals.

3) Finally, assess the competencies of your candidate for each role (per table 4.4).

Table 4.4.

Competency	Competency indicators	Rating	Notes
Decision making	❑ Uses advanced thinking to make decisions ❑ Makes effective decisions on a daily basis ❑ Selects the best options available when facing difficult scenarios	❑ Excellent ❑ Very good ❑ Good ❑ Poor	
Teamwork	❑ Communicates effectively with other team members ❑ Able to cooperate with colleagues and motivate project members ❑ Understands what others need, acknowledges their work, and gives support	❑ Excellent ❑ Very good ❑ Good ❑ Poor	

Competency Coverage Model

The competency coverage model focuses on which screening activities will best assess the competencies of your candidate. Screening activities include résumés or CVs, telephone calls, tests, interviews, and reference checks. The matrix in table 4.5 is adapted from Mckay and Simpson (2013) and demonstrates the two screening techniques that best evaluate each competency required for a position.

Table 4.5.

Position	Competencies	Screening technique				
		Résumé/CV	Test	Telephone call	Interview	Reference check
Chief HR Officer	Coaching				X	X
	Change management				X	X
	Continued learning	X		X		
Sales Manager	Client focus				X	X
	Product knowledge		X		X	
	Sales skills		X		X	
Secretary	Communication		X	X		
	Computer skills	X	X			
	Collaboration			X	X	

Note: Each role can have more than three competencies, and you can use more than two screening techniques to assess each competency.

The competency coverage model is a solid recruitment planning tool. It allows you to predict which screening activities will successfully assess competencies. I highly recommend following these steps:

1) List all the positions you have to fill.
2) List competencies for each position.
3) Make your best predictions (based on experience or historical data).

Table 4.5 explains that the chief human resource officer (CHRO) role has three main competencies—coaching, change management, and continued learning. You are capable of evaluating change management and coaching by conducting interviews and reference checks. You can evaluate the continued learning competency from the candidate's résumé and telephone screening because a résumé will show any pursuit of advanced education or professional certificates. You can also ask about this during the telephone screening.

Competencies and Strategic Objectives

Those in talent acquisition will have to plan their recruitment strategies to connect competencies to their companies' goals. You should identify core competencies that are vital for the business and impact the business's bottom line.

With a clear idea of the company's vision and mission, you will have to ask what critical competencies the company has and what main competencies it needs to acquire. Therefore, depending on the business, the industry, and the short- or long-term objectives, a recruiter will have to identify these competencies accordingly:

- For a company whose objective is to maximize profit and increase sales, core or critical competencies might be operational excellence, communication initiative, sales skills, and customer orientation.
- For a company whose objective is the development of new products, core or critical competencies might be managing change, teamwork and cooperation, creativity and innovation, product knowledge, analytical thinking, and customer orientation.
- For a company whose objective is to have the best working environment, core or critical competencies might be managing change, teamwork and cooperation, communication, emotional intelligence, effective leadership, and coaching and mentoring.
- If a company aims to lead through technological innovation, its core or critical competencies might be systems thinking, teamwork and cooperation, creativity and innovation, technical expertise, problem solving, and dedication.

- If a start-up aims to manufacture plastics and gain a huge market share, its core or critical competencies might be entrepreneurship, teamwork and cooperation, managing performance, continued learning, manufacturing expertise, and project management.

Recruitment for Nonrecruiters

In conclusion, I highly recommend crafting a recruitment tool kit with practical recruitment material, or a minicourse to transfer knowledge to other departments within the company. Some might create a YouTube channel or circulate recruitment training material to other departments. Some companies might have the time and ability to conduct recruitment sessions for people outside of the recruitment team.

HR knowledge should not be limited to HR professionals. For example, department heads frequently conduct interviews to hire staff for their departments. The question is whether they know how to conduct a competency-based interview. Do they know how to probe? Do they know how to avoid the interview biases explained earlier? I personally don't think so.

From my point of view, the decision to hire should be a mutual decision between the recruitment team and other departments. Successful hiring requires the support of all, and it requires the professional use of recruitment practices.

Other departments (legal, IT, finance, etc.) should conduct recruitment methods, including structured or competency-based interviews. For example, nowadays finance for nonfinance managers is a mandatory course for all department heads—regardless of their backgrounds. I think everyone should pay attention to human capital too. The least anyone can do is circulate online recruitment material covering an interesting subject, such as competency-based interviews. This might just improve the overall selection and talent acquisition within your company.

QUESTIONS

1) How do you define "talent"?

2) How do you define "man-power planning"?

3) Which position was the most difficult for you to fill? Why was it difficult, and what did you do to fill the role?

4) Company YX aims to hire thirty positions during 2016. Fifteen positions have been filled. What is the ratio of vacant versus filled positions?

5) What are the five main elements of the five *S* recruitment model? Do you apply all of them?

6) Which recruitment technique in the book resonated with you the most? Why?

7) How do you calculate the nationalization percentage? What methods do you plan to use to increase your company's nationalization percentage?

8) Does your company audit your recruitment department? If so, how frequently?

9) You decide to hire a finance manager. What competencies will you select from the competency list in chapter 4 to evaluate candidates?

10) Which talent acquisition model will you start applying immediately? How will you do so?

BIBLIOGRAPHY

Australian Public Service Commission. 2015. "Span of Control." *APS Human Capital Matters* 4 (May): 1–8.
http://webcache.googleusercontent.com/search?q=cache:483K2Cg08lIJ:www.apsc.gov.au/__data/assets/word_doc/0005/65615/Human-Capital-Matters-Vol-4-2015-Span-of-Control.DOCX+&cd=1&hl=en&ct=clnk&gl=sa

Bogardus, Anne M. 2009. *PHR/SPHR: Professional in Human Resources Certification Study Guide*, 3rd ed. Indianapolis, IN: Wiley.

Caruth, Donald L., and Gail D. Handlogten. 1997. *Staffing the Contemporary Organization: A Guide to Planning, Recruiting, and Selecting for Human Resource Professionals*. Westport, CT: Quorum.

Floros, Panos, and Samir Khayzaran. 2015. "*Why Strategic Workforce Planning?*" Paper presented at Hay Group interactive session, September, Riyadh, Saudi Arabia.

Gallardo-Gallardo, Eva, Nicky Dries, and Tomas F. Gonzalez-Cruz. 2013. "What Is the Meaning of 'Talent' in the World of Work?" *Human Resource Management Review* 23: 290–300.

Hay Group. 2013. "State of Idaho: Benefits Analysis & Total Compensation Review." Hay Group.
http://dhr.idaho.gov/PDF%20documents/Compensation/HayGroupTotCompReportJan2013.pdf

Hay Group. 2009. "Making Sure Your Organization Structures Stack Up." Hay Group.
http://www.haygroup.com/Downloads/us/misc/Best_Organization_Design_Practices_-_Hay_Group_NA_Chemicals_Industry_Forum_October_2009.pdf

Mckay, Lorraine, and Suzanne Simpson. 2013 "Advanced Competency-Based Talent Management." Paper presented at Human Resource Systems Group training, April, Dubai, UAE.

Spencer, Lyle M., and Signe M. Spencer. 1993. *Competence at Work: Models for Superior Performance*. New York: Wiley.

Ulrich, Dave, and Norm Smallwood. "What Is Talent?" *Executive White Paper Series* (n.d.), 1–7. https://michiganross.umich.edu/sites/default/files/uploads/RTIA/pdfs/dulrich_wp_what_is_talent.pdf

Made in the USA
Middletown, DE
04 October 2018

...essing: REM sleep is crucial for processing
...emotions. It helps integrate emotional
...ducing emotional reactivity and enhancing
...lience.
...Memory: REM sleep plays a significant role in
...ation of procedural and spatial memories,
...rning and cognitive function.

...of Sleep

...component of overall health, regulated by two
...anisms: the circadian rhythm and the
...adenosine system. Understanding these
...helps us appreciate how our bodies control the
...ocesses of sleep and wakefulness.

...Rhythm and Sleep Regulation

...dian rhythm, derived from the Latin "circa diem"
..."around a day," is a natural, internal process that
...s the sleep-wake cycle and other physiological
...ses. This rhythm follows a roughly 24-hour cycle and is
...ced by external environmental cues known as
...bers, with light being the most influential.

Brain Waves and Phases of Sleep

1. **Beta Waves**: These are high-frequency, low-amplitude brain waves typically present when we are awake and engaged in active thought processes. They signify a state of alertness and active cognitive engagement.
2. **Alpha Waves**: These waves occur when we are awake but in a relaxed state, such as during meditation or just before falling asleep. Alpha waves indicate a state of calm and restful alertness.
3. **Theta Waves**: These waves are seen during the lighter stages of non-REM sleep (NREM sleep). Theta waves are slower in frequency and indicate a transition from wakefulness to sleep.
4. **Sleep Spindles and K-Complexes**: These unique brain wave patterns are characteristic of Stage 2 NREM sleep. Sleep spindles are bursts of rapid, rhythmic brain activity, while K-complexes are large waves that react to external stimuli, helping to protect sleep and aid in memory consolidation.
5. Delta Waves: These slow, high-amplitude waves dominate Stage 3 NREM sleep, also known as slow-wave sleep (SWS). Delta waves are crucial for the deepest, most restorative stages of sleep.

5. **REM sleep brain waves**: REM (Rapid Eye Movement) sleep is a distinct stage of sleep characterised by specific patterns of brain activity, which are identifiable through electroencephalography (EEG). During REM sleep, the brain exhibits a unique combination of high-frequency, low-amplitude waves that closely resemble the awake state.

The 90-Minute Sleep Cycle

Sleep cycles typically last about 90 minutes and consist of light sleep, slow-wave sleep, and REM sleep. Each stage plays a vital role in the restorative processes of the body and brain.

1. **Light Sleep**: This phase includes both Stage 1 and Stage 2 of NREM sleep. During light sleep, the body begins to relax, heart rate slows, and body temperature drops. Brain waves transition from alpha to theta waves, and sleep spindles and K-complexes occur, signaling the brain's efforts to process memories and maintain sleep stability.

2. **Slow-Wave Sleep (SWS)**: Also known as deep sleep, this phase is characterized by delta waves. SWS is crucial for physical restoration, growth, and repair. It helps replenish glial glycogen stores, supports immune function, and facilitates the clearance of brain waste through the glymphatic system, reducing the risk of neurodegenerative diseases such as Alzheimer's.

3. **REM Sleep**: REM
   cycle an
   n
   mu
   grou
   learnir
   emotior
   enhancing

Role and Func
Slow-Wave Sleep

- **Homeostatic B**
  body's homeosta
  regeneration of tiss
  and restoring energy
- **Memory Consolidatio**
  during SWS are involve
  memories, facilitating the
  short-term to long-term st
- **Glymphatic System Functio**
  glymphatic system during SW
  metabolic waste products from
  of neurodegenerative diseases.

REM Sleep

- **Emotional Proc**
  and regulating
  experiences, re
  emotional res
- **Learning and**
  the consolid
  aiding in lea

Regulation

Sleep is a vita
primary mech
homeostatic
mechanism
complex pr

Circadia

The circa
meaning
regulate
proces
influer
zeitge

- **Suprachiasmatic Nucleus (SCN):** At the core of circadian rhythm regulation is the suprachiasmatic nucleus (SCN), a small region in the hypothalamus. The SCN is often referred to as the body's master clock. It receives direct input from the eyes, allowing it to synchronize the body's internal clock with the external light environment.
- **Role of Light:** Light exposure plays a critical role in regulating the circadian rhythm. When light enters the eyes, it is detected by photoreceptors and signals are sent to the SCN. The SCN then adjusts the production of melatonin, a hormone produced by the pineal gland that promotes sleep. During the day, light exposure inhibits melatonin production, promoting wakefulness. As light decreases in the evening, melatonin levels rise, signalling to the body that it is time to sleep.

- **Melatonin Production:** Melatonin is sometimes called the "sleep hormone." It helps regulate sleep by signalling to the body that it is time to prepare for sleep. The timing and amount of melatonin production are influenced by the SCN and the amount of light exposure.

The Homeostatic-Adenosine System and Sleep Pressure

Another crucial mechanism in sleep regulation is the homeostati-adenosine system, which helps build sleep pressure throughout the day.

- **Adenosine Accumulation**: adenosine is a neurotransmitter that accumulates in the brain during wakefulness. As the day progresses, adenosine levels gradually increase, creating a pressure to sleep. This process is often referred to as sleep homeostasis or sleep pressure.
- **Sleep Pressure and Wakefulness**: the longer we are awake, the more adenosine builds up, making us feel increasingly sleepy. This buildup of adenosine helps ensure that we eventually fall asleep and get the rest we need.
- **Clearing Adenosine During Sleep**: during sleep, especially during slow-wave sleep (SWS), adenosine levels decrease, relieving sleep pressure and allowing us to wake up feeling refreshed. This cycle of adenosine buildup and clearance is essential for maintaining a balanced sleep-wake cycle.

The Impact of Caffeine on Sleep

Caffeine is one of the most widely consumed stimulants, commonly used to combat sleepiness and enhance alertness, particularly among shift workers and those needing to stay awake for extended periods. However, its effects on sleep can be profound due to its action as an adenosine receptor antagonist.

How Caffeine Works

Adenosine is an inhibitory neurotransmitter that accumulates in the brain throughout the day, promoting sleepiness by evening. It is a key component of the homeostatic regulation of sleep, helping to balance sleep and wakefulness. Caffeine works by blocking the action of adenosine, which delays the onset of sleep and can disrupt normal sleep patterns. By binding to adenosine receptors, caffeine prevents the feelings of drowsiness that adenosine would typically induce.

Half-Life of Caffeine

The half-life of caffeine—the time it takes for the body to eliminate half of the caffeine consumed—varies between individuals but generally ranges from 3 to 5 hours. This means that if you drink a cup of coffee containing 100 mg of caffeine, after 3 to 5 hours, 50 mg of caffeine will still be in your system. The effects of caffeine can last much longer, potentially affecting sleep quality if consumed too late in the day.

For optimal sleep hygiene, it is generally recommended to avoid caffeine consumption at least 6 to 8 hours before bedtime. This precaution helps ensure that caffeine's stimulating effects have diminished, reducing the risk of delayed sleep onset and disturbed sleep.

The Post-Caffeine Crash

While caffeine temporarily blocks adenosine and enhances alertness, it does not eliminate the underlying buildup of adenosine. Once the effects of caffeine wear off, the accumulated adenosine floods the receptors, often resulting in a "post-caffeine crash." This crash is characterized by sudden fatigue and drowsiness, which can be particularly pronounced if caffeine consumption was high. This phenomenon underscores the temporary nature of caffeine's benefits and the body's eventual need to process and respond to accumulated adenosine.

Implications for Sleep

Understanding the pharmacokinetics of caffeine is crucial for managing its impact on sleep. Consuming caffeine late in the day can significantly impair the ability to fall asleep and achieve restful sleep. This disruption can lead to a cycle of increased caffeine consumption to combat daytime fatigue, further exacerbating sleep disturbances.

Additionally, while caffeine may enhance alertness temporarily, reliance on it can mask underlying sleep deficits, leading to a reliance on the stimulant and further disrupting natural sleep patterns.

Individual Variations

The effect of caffeine varies among individuals. Some people metabolize caffeine quickly due to genetic variations, while others, particularly smokers, may require higher doses due to the induced hepatic enzymes that metabolize caffeine more rapidly. Understanding individual responses to caffeine is important for providing personalized advice on its consumption.

Interplay Between Circadian Rhythm and Adenosine System

The circadian rhythm and adenosine system work together to regulate sleep and wakefulness:

- **Circadian Rhythm**: Regulates the timing of sleep and wakefulness, aligning our sleep patterns with the external environment.
- **Adenosine System**: Builds sleep pressure throughout the day, ensuring that we feel sleepy after a prolonged period of wakefulness.

This interplay ensures that we not only sleep at the right times but also get the right amount of sleep needed for optimal health and functioning. Disruptions to either system, such as irregular light exposure or prolonged wakefulness, can lead to sleep disorders and negatively impact overall health.

The Importance of Sleep Quantity and Quality

The duration and quality of sleep are essential for overall health. Adults typically need about seven to nine hours of sleep per night. It is a misnomer that older people need less sleep: older individuals often are not able to achieve the same amount of sleep as they did when younger. Chronic sleep deprivation can impair cognitive functions, emotional stability, and immune response, highlighting the importance of adequate sleep for maintaining optimal health. Quality sleep involves both sufficient duration and proper progression through the sleep stages, ensuring that both the body and mind are fully rejuvenated.

Immune Function and Sleep

Sleep plays a vital role in maintaining a robust immune system. Sleep deprivation has been linked to a decrease in the production of natural killer cells, which are essential for combating infections and potentially tumor cells. Studies indicate that individuals restricted to only four hours of sleep show a 72% reduction in these cells. Additionally, sleep deprivation is associated with increased levels of inflammatory proteins, which may elevate the risk of cardiovascular diseases and strokes, especially in shift workers who often experience disrupted sleep patterns.

The Endocrine Impact of Sleep

Hormonal regulation is another critical function influenced by sleep. For instance, the hormone ghrelin, which stimulates appetite, increases in individuals who are sleep deprived. Consequently, sleep deprivation can lead to higher calorie intake and weight gain. Furthermore, prolonged sleep deprivation elevates cortisol levels, a stress hormone that can increase blood sugar levels, posing a risk for those with diabetes. The interplay between these hormones and sleep demonstrates the intricate balance required for maintaining metabolic health.

Mental Health Effects of Sleep

- **Maintenance of Normal Mood and Resolution of Mood Disorders:** Adequate sleep is essential for maintaining emotional stability and resolving mood disorders such as depression and anxiety. During sleep, especially REM sleep, the brain processes emotional experiences, helping to regulate mood.
- **Processing of Trauma:** Sleep, particularly REM sleep, plays a critical role in processing traumatic experiences, reducing the emotional impact of trauma and aiding in the treatment of PTSD.

Psychological Effects of Sleep Deprivation

Sleep is essential for maintaining various physiological and psychological functions. When we don't get enough sleep, it can have profound effects on our mental health and cognitive abilities. Here, we explore the psychological effects of sleep deprivation and the mechanisms behind them.

Reduced Slow-Wave Sleep (SWS)

Slow-wave sleep (SWS) is crucial for physical restoration, immune function, and memory consolidation. When sleep is deprived, the amount of SWS decreases, impairing the body's ability to repair tissues, maintain immune health, and consolidate memories. This reduction in SWS can lead to a weakened immune system and difficulty remembering and learning new information.

Reduced REM Sleep

REM sleep is vital for emotional regulation, memory processing, and learning. A decrease in REM sleep due to sleep deprivation leads to difficulties in managing emotions, processing experiences, and integrating memories. This can result in increased emotional instability and difficulty in retaining and recalling information.

Brain-Derived Neurotrophic Factor (BDNF) Reduction

Sleep deprivation reduces levels of Brain-Derived Neurotrophic Factor (BDNF), a protein essential for brain health. BDNF supports the growth and differentiation of new neurons and synapses, which are critical for learning and memory. Reduced BDNF levels impair cognitive functions, making it harder to learn new information and form long-term memories.

Memory Impairment

One of the most significant effects of sleep deprivation is memory impairment. Lack of sleep disrupts the brain's ability to consolidate short-term memories into long-term storage. This disruption leads to forgetfulness and difficulty in learning new concepts or skills, as the brain cannot effectively process and store information.

Learning Impairment

Sleep is crucial for cognitive functions such as attention, reasoning, and problem-solving. Without adequate sleep, these abilities suffer, leading to impaired learning. Sleep deprivation negatively impacts concentration, making it challenging to focus on tasks and solve problems efficiently.

Emotional Distress

Poor sleep increases irritability, stress, and emotional instability. When we don't get enough sleep, our ability to regulate emotions is compromised, contributing to conditions like depression and anxiety. The lack of restorative sleep amplifies stress responses, making it harder to cope with daily challenges.

Processing Sleep and Fear Extinction

Adequate sleep, particularly REM sleep, is necessary for the brain to process fears and reduce anxiety. During REM sleep, the brain helps extinguish fear responses to previously traumatic stimuli. Without sufficient REM sleep, this process is disrupted, leading to heightened anxiety and an inability to move past traumatic experiences.

Social Morality and Social Cues

Sleep deprivation affects our ability to read social cues and respond appropriately. This impairment can lead to difficulties in social interactions and moral decision-making. People who are sleep-deprived may misinterpret others' emotions and intentions, leading to misunderstandings and inappropriate social behaviour.

Decreased Alertness

Reduced sleep decreases alertness and reaction time, affecting daily performance and increasing the risk of accidents. Whether driving, operating machinery, or performing everyday tasks, a lack of sleep can lead to slower response times and impaired judgment, raising the likelihood of mistakes and accidents.

Conclusion

Understanding the multifaceted nature of sleep underscores its vital role in overall health. From brain housekeeping and emotional regulation to immune function and hormonal balance, sleep is integral to numerous physiological processes. Ensuring adequate and quality sleep is essential for maintaining physical and mental well-being, highlighting the need for health professionals to emphasize the importance of sleep in their practice.

Chapter 2: Sleep Phase Disorders

Understanding Sleep Phase Disorders

Sleep phase disorders are disruptions in the body's natural sleep-wake cycle, often categorized into two main types: delayed sleep phase disorder (DSPD) and advanced sleep phase disorder (ASPD). These disorders can significantly impact daily functioning and are commonly observed at the extremes of age, affecting teenagers and the elderly differently.

Delayed Sleep Phase Disorder (DSPD)

DSPD is characterised by a natural sleep-wake cycle that is longer than 24 hours. This condition is prevalent among teenagers who tend to fall asleep late and wake up late. The body's internal clock, or circadian rhythm, in these individuals runs on a delayed schedule, making it challenging to align with conventional societal norms of early sleep and early wake times. Teens with DSPD often struggle with morning commitments such as school or work, leading to sleep deprivation and its associated consequences.

Advanced Sleep Phase Disorder (ASPD)

ASPD, on the other hand, typically affects the elderly. In this disorder, the circadian rhythm is shorter than 24 hours, leading individuals to fall asleep early in the evening and wake up very early in the morning. This shift can disrupt social activities and may cause difficulties in staying awake during desired hours. Individuals with ASPD often experience difficulty in maintaining social engagements or evening activities, which can lead to feelings of isolation and frustration.

The Role of Circadian Rhythm

The circadian rhythm, which governs the sleep-wake cycle, is influenced by external environmental cues, primarily light. In individuals with DSPD or ASPD, this rhythm is misaligned with the 24-hour day-night cycle. In the absence of external cues, such as sunlight, the natural sleep-wake cycle can diverge significantly from the standard 24-hour period. This misalignment can lead to chronic sleep issues and impact overall health and well-being.

The Challenge of Jet Lag

Jet lag is a common phenomenon experienced when crossing more than three time zones, causing a misalignment between the body's internal clock and the new local time. The severity of jet lag depends on the direction of travel:

- **Eastward Travel:** Often results in advanced sleep phase, making it harder to fall asleep and wake up early.
- **Westward Travel:** Generally easier to adapt to, as it involves delaying sleep, which aligns more naturally with the body's ability to stay awake longer.

Managing Jet Lag

Effective management of jet lag involves strategic light exposure and melatonin use:

- **Eastward Travel:** Exposure to light early in the day and melatonin at night can help adjust the sleep phase.
- **Westward Travel:** Light exposure later in the day can help delay sleep, making it easier to stay awake until the new local bedtime.

Hydration and Nutrition

Maintaining proper hydration and following a balanced diet can also mitigate the effects of jet lag. Avoiding heavy, salty foods and staying hydrated helps in maintaining overall well-being during travel. Eating meals at times that align with the destination's schedule can also help reset the body's internal clock more quickly.

Practical Advice for Health Professionals

Assessing Underlying Conditions Affecting Sleep

Before prescribing treatments like melatonin or light therapy, it is crucial to rule out underlying conditions that can affect sleep. Addressing these conditions directly can often improve sleep without the need for additional interventions. Below are some common conditions that should be considered when assessing sleep disturbances.

Mood Disorders

- **Depression**: Depression can significantly disrupt sleep, leading to insomnia or hypersomnia. People with depression often experience early morning awakenings and difficulty falling asleep. Treating depression with therapy or medication can improve sleep quality.
- **Anxiety**: Anxiety disorders are closely linked with sleep problems, often causing difficulty falling or staying asleep. Chronic anxiety increases arousal and worry, interfering with the relaxation necessary for sleep. Addressing anxiety through cognitive-behavioral therapy (CBT) or medication can lead to better sleep outcomes.

Sleep Apnea

Sleep apnea is a condition where breathing repeatedly stops and starts during sleep. This leads to fragmented sleep and reduced oxygen supply to the body, causing daytime fatigue and other health issues. Diagnosing and treating sleep apnea with continuous positive airway pressure (CPAP) therapy or other interventions can restore normal sleep patterns.

Periodic Limb Movement Disorder (PLMD) and Restless Legs Syndrome (RLS)

- **PLMD**: This disorder involves involuntary limb movements during sleep, often leading to frequent awakenings and poor sleep quality. It can be diagnosed through a sleep study and treated with medications.
- **RLS**: Restless Legs Syndrome is characterized by an irresistible urge to move the legs, usually due to uncomfortable sensations. These symptoms often worsen in the evening, making it difficult to fall asleep. RLS can be associated with iron deficiency, so addressing this deficiency can alleviate symptoms and improve sleep.

Narcolepsy

Narcolepsy is a neurological disorder characterized by excessive daytime sleepiness and sudden sleep attacks. It often includes other symptoms such as cataplexy (sudden loss of muscle tone), sleep paralysis, and hallucinations. Managing narcolepsy typically involves medications and lifestyle changes to help regulate sleep-wake cycles.

Shift Work Sleep Disorder

Shift work, especially night shifts, can disrupt the body's natural circadian rhythm, leading to difficulty falling asleep and maintaining regular sleep patterns. This disorder often results in insomnia or excessive sleepiness. Strategies to manage shift work sleep disorder include:

- **Light Therapy**: Using bright light exposure at strategic times to help reset the circadian rhythm.
- **Melatonin**: Supplementing with melatonin to help signal the body that it is time to sleep.
- **Sleep Hygiene**: Implementing strict sleep hygiene practices to create a conducive sleep environment despite irregular work hours.

A comprehensive assessment of underlying conditions is essential for effectively addressing sleep disturbances. By identifying and treating conditions such as mood and anxiety disorders, sleep apnea, PLMD, RLS, narcolepsy, and shift work sleep disorder, healthcare providers can improve sleep quality without resorting to secondary treatments like melatonin or light therapy. This holistic approach ensures that the root causes of sleep problems are addressed, leading to more sustainable and long-term sleep health.

Sleep Hygiene Assessment

A comprehensive sleep hygiene assessment includes evaluating factors that can be recalled by the mnemonic "WEANS":

- **Wind Down (W):** Failure to wind down before bedtime can hinder the ability to fall asleep.
- **Efficiency (E):** Reduced sleep efficiency, or the percentage of time spent asleep while in bed, can indicate poor sleep quality.
- **Activity (A):** Using the bedroom for unsanctioned activities, such as watching TV or working, can disrupt the association between the bed and sleep.
- **Naps (N):** Daytime naps exceeding 30 minutes can interfere with nighttime sleep.
- **Substances (S):** Consumption of alcohol or caffeine within 3 hours of bedtime can disrupt sleep.

Comprehensive Management of Sleep Phase Disorders

Effective management of sleep phase disorders involves a holistic approach that considers both sleep and wake phases. Combining melatonin therapy with strategic light exposure and lifestyle modifications can significantly improve sleep patterns. Educating patients on these practices is essential for long-term success.

Melatonin Therapy

Melatonin, a hormone produced by the pineal gland, plays a crucial role in regulating sleep. It can be used therapeutically to adjust the sleep phase. For individuals with DSPD, melatonin can be taken in the evening to promote earlier sleep onset. Conversely, those with ASPD might take melatonin in the morning to delay the sleep phase. Proper dosing and timing are critical to the effectiveness of melatonin therapy, and it is often used in conjunction with other treatments.

Light Therapy

Light exposure is a powerful tool for adjusting the circadian rhythm. Early morning light exposure can help individuals with DSPD advance their sleep-wake cycle to societal norms. For those with ASPD, controlled light exposure later in the morning can help delay their sleep phase, enabling them to stay awake and active later into the evening. Bright light therapy boxes are often used to provide the necessary light exposure, especially in regions with limited natural sunlight during certain seasons.

- **Morning Sunlight**: Exposure to natural light in the morning helps reset the circadian rhythm and promote wakefulness during the day.
- **Evening Light**: Reducing exposure to artificial light in the evening, particularly blue light from screens, helps increase melatonin production and prepare the body for sleep.

Chronotherapy

Chronotherapy involves gradually adjusting the sleep-wake times to shift the circadian rhythm. This method can be particularly useful but requires careful supervision by a sleep physician or psychologist. The process involves incrementally delaying sleep time each night until the desired sleep schedule is achieved. This gradual adjustment helps in realigning the internal clock without causing significant sleep deprivation. Chronotherapy can be a complex process, requiring commitment and consistency from the patient.

Patient Education and Sleep Hygiene

Educating patients about proper sleep hygiene is crucial for maintaining a healthy circadian rhythm and improving sleep quality. The following guidelines should be communicated to all patients:

1. **Protect Sleep Opportunity**: Ensure at least eight hours of sleep opportunity each day. Maintain regular bedtimes and wake times throughout the week, including weekends. Lying in for more than an hour beyond the usual wake-up time on weekends may indicate an irrecoverable sleep debt during the week.
2. **Regular Exercise**: Exercise daily but avoid vigorous activity within three hours of bedtime. Physical activity can promote better sleep, but exercising too close to bedtime may have a stimulating effect.
3. **Caffeine and Nicotine**: Avoid caffeine and cigarettes, especially in the afternoon and evening, as both are stimulants that can impair sleep.
4. **Heavy Meals and Alcohol**: Avoid heavy meals at night, with at least one hour, preferably four hours, between the last meal and bedtime. Also, avoid alcohol within six hours of bedtime as it can disrupt sleep architecture.
5. Medication Review: Avoid medications that have an adverse effect on sleep. A thorough review of current medications with a healthcare provider may be necessary.
6. Daytime Napping: Avoid napping after 3 pm. If unable to fall asleep at night, completely avoid napping to ensure sufficient sleep pressure builds up for the next night.

7. **Wind-Down Routine**: Establish a 30 to 60-minute wind-down routine before bed. This could include activities such as reading, taking a warm bath, or practicing relaxation techniques.

8. **Optimal Bedroom Environment**: Ensure the bedroom is completely dark and free of technology. LED blue light significantly impairs melatonin secretion. The bedroom temperature should be lower at night, with an optimal range between 12 and 16 degrees Celsius.

9. **Consistent Wake Time**: Rise at the same time every day, including weekends. Exposure to morning sunlight outdoors is beneficial, as natural light helps switch off nighttime melatonin secretion and triggers a delayed secretion 12 to 14 hours later.

10. **Managing Sleeplessness**: If unable to fall asleep within 30 minutes, get up and engage in a relaxing, non-stimulating activity until feeling sufficiently tired to return to bed. Regardless of delayed return to bed, rise at the usual time the next morning.

Conclusion

Comprehensive management of sleep phase disorders requires a multifaceted approach that includes melatonin therapy, strategic light exposure, and lifestyle modifications. Educating patients on proper sleep hygiene practices is crucial for achieving and maintaining healthy sleep patterns. By implementing these strategies, patients can improve their sleep quality and overall well-being.

Chapter 3:
The COLTE Mnemonic and Sleep

Introduction to COLTE

The COLTE mnemonic is an essential tool for understanding the various factors that influence our sleep patterns. It stands for Carbohydrates (C), Osmolality (O), Light (L), Temperature (T), and Exercise (E). Light is the most important factor, but all play a crucial role in regulating sleep and maintaining a healthy circadian rhythm.

Carbohydrates

High Concentrations of Tryptophan: tryptophan, an amino acid, enters the brain more easily after consuming carbohydrates, facilitating the production of serotonin and melatonin, both of which promote sleep.

Carbohydrates significantly impact sleep by influencing hormonal activity in the brain. When we consume a carbohydrate-rich meal, insulin is released, which lowers the levels of most amino acids in the bloodstream except for tryptophan. Tryptophan is essential for producing serotonin and melatonin, both of which promote sleep. Additionally, carbohydrates can affect orexin, a hormone that promotes wakefulness. Sugars from carbohydrates bind to orexin cells, decreasing their activity and contributing to sleepiness.

Timing and Types of Meals

To optimize sleep, it is recommended to consume a carbohydrate-rich meal approximately four hours before bedtime. This allows sufficient time for digestion and the hormonal changes necessary for sleep onset. The timing of the meal is crucial because eating too close to bedtime can disrupt sleep, while eating too early may not provide the same benefits. Including complex carbohydrates such as whole grains, fruits, and vegetables can also help maintain steady blood sugar levels, further promoting restful sleep.

Osmolality

Osmolality refers to the balance of salts and water in the body. Maintaining proper osmolality is critical for sleep. High sodium intake or dehydration can interfere with the body's ability to lower core temperature, a necessary process for initiating sleep. During the early phase of sleep, the body reduces core temperature through peripheral vasodilation, which is impaired by high osmolality. Thus, avoiding high-sodium foods and ensuring adequate hydration are essential for promoting restful sleep.

Practical Tips for Osmolality Balance

To maintain optimal osmolality for sleep, individuals should:

- Drink plenty of water throughout the day, especially in the hours leading up to bedtime.
- Avoid consuming high-sodium foods, particularly in the evening.
- Incorporate foods rich in potassium, such as bananas and leafy greens, which help balance sodium levels.

Light

Light within 2-3 Hours of Waking: morning light exposure helps regulate the circadian rhythm and improves alertness and mood throughout the day.

Sky Gazing in the Morning

Looking at the sky (not the sun) in the morning is one of the most effective ways to receive adequate light exposure, helping to reset the circadian rhythm and improve sleep quality. Light intensity from even an overcast day far exceeds any indoor lighting as can be seen from the comparison figures below.

Light Intensity Comparisons:

- **Bright Sunny Day:** 100,000 lux
- **Cloudy Day:** 25,000 lux
- **Overcast Rainy Day:** 10,000 lux
- **Industrial Lighting:** 5,000 lux
- **Office Lighting:** 500 lux
- **Home Lighting:** 50 lux
- **Street Lighting:** 20 lux
- **Moonlight:** 1 lux

Guidelines for Light Exposure

Light is the most potent regulator of the circadian rhythm, significantly influencing sleep patterns and overall health. Effective management of light exposure involves strategies for maximizing beneficial light in the morning and minimizing disruptive light in the evening. Below are some guidelines for light exposure:

Morning Light Exposure

1. **Wear Glasses but Not Sunglasses**: sunglasses can block essential light needed to regulate the circadian rhythm, whereas for those who need them, corrective glasses focus light onto the retina.
2. **Seek Early Morning Sunlight**: exposure to natural light in the morning helps set the body's internal clock, promoting alertness and preparing the body for the day. Aim to spend at least 20-30 minutes outside shortly after waking up.
3. **Protect Your Eyes**: if your eyes hurt or vision becomes blurred during light exposure, stop immediately and consult your doctor. It's essential to protect your eye health while benefiting from light exposure.

Evening Light Management

1. **Avoid Blue Light in the Evening**: blue light, commonly emitted by screens (phones, tablets, computers) and certain artificial lighting, suppresses melatonin secretion, increases heart rate, blood pressure, and core body temperature, all of which counteract the physiological changes needed for sleep.

2. **Create a Dark Sleep Environment**: to support melatonin production, ensure your sleep environment is dark. Use blackout curtains to block external light and remove or cover sources of artificial light in the bedroom.

3. **Use Dim, Warm Lighting**: in the evening, switch to dim, warm lighting to mimic the natural decrease in light intensity. This helps signal to your body that it's time to wind down and prepare for sleep.

4. **Blue Light Filters:**utilise blue light filters on electronic devices to reduce the impact of screen exposure before bedtime. These filters can be installed as apps or built into the settings of most modern devices.

5. Avoid Screens Before Bed: limit screen time at least an hour before bedtime to minimize blue light exposure. Engage in relaxing activities such as reading a book (preferably a physical one rather than an e-book), listening to calming music, or practicing mindfulness meditation.

6. **Moonlight and Firelight**: Unlike blue light, moonlight and the red light of a fire do not suppress melatonin production or impair sleep. If you need some light in the evening, consider using red or amber lights, which are less likely to disrupt your sleep cycle.

By managing light exposure effectively, individuals can significantly improve their sleep patterns and overall well-being. Early morning sunlight helps set the body's internal clock, while reducing blue light exposure in the evening supports melatonin production and prepares the body for restful sleep. Incorporating these guidelines into daily routines can enhance sleep hygiene and promote better health.

Temperature and Sleep: Optimizing Your Sleep Environment

Temperature regulation is a critical factor in sleep initiation and maintenance. The body's core temperature naturally drops during the first half of sleep, which is facilitated by the dilation of blood vessels in the hands and feet. A comfortable room temperature supports the body's efforts to cool down, ensuring a restful night's sleep.

Optimal Room Temperature for Sleep

The ideal room temperature for sleep is between 15 to 19 degrees Celsius (59 to 66 degrees Fahrenheit). Maintaining this temperature helps the body cool down, facilitating the onset of sleep. A cooler environment aligns with the body's natural temperature drop during sleep, promoting deeper and more restorative rest.

Paradoxical Thermic Effect

The paradoxical thermic effect refers to how different temperature exposures can influence the body's core temperature and subsequent physiological responses:

- **Cold Showers in the Morning**: taking a cold shower in the morning can increase the rate of body temperature rise, promoting wakefulness. Cold exposure causes thermogenesis by shivering, which generates heat and helps to elevate the body's core temperature. This rise in body temperature signals to the body that it is time to be alert and awake.
- **Warm Showers at Night**: conversely, taking a warm shower at night can help relax the body and prepare it for sleep. Warm exposure causes peripheral vasodilation, which facilitates the loss of heat through the extremities, resulting in the cooling of the core body temperature. This cooling effect promotes the onset of sleep by aligning with the body's natural nighttime temperature drop.

Practices for Temperature Regulation

To optimise sleep, consider incorporating the following practices for effective temperature regulation:

1. **Warm Bath or Beverage Before Bed:** taking a warm bath or drinking a warm beverage before bed can temporarily raise core body temperature. This increase in temperature promotes peripheral vasodilation, helping to cool the core body temperature as the body loses heat through the extremities. This process aids in relaxing the body and preparing it for sleep.

2. **Maintain an Ideal Room Temperature:** ensure that the sleep environment is not too hot or too cold. The ideal room temperature for sleep is typically between 60-67 degrees Fahrenheit (15-19 degrees Celsius). Adjust the thermostat or use fans or heaters as needed to achieve this temperature range.

3. **Breathable Sleepwear and Appropriate Bedding:** wearing breathable sleepwear and using appropriate bedding can help regulate body temperature throughout the night. Natural fabrics like cotton and linen allow for better air circulation, preventing overheating. Layering blankets allows for easy adjustments to maintain comfort.

4. **Cool Environment for Better Sleep:** keeping the sleep environment cool can enhance sleep quality. Consider using a fan or air conditioning to maintain a steady, cool temperature. Avoid heavy, heat-retaining bedding that can cause overheating during the night.

5. **Avoiding Extremes:** while it's important to stay cool, extremely cold environments can also be disruptive. Finding a balance that supports the body's natural thermoregulation processes is key to optimal sleep.

Temperature regulation is a vital aspect of achieving and maintaining high-quality sleep. By understanding and applying principles like the paradoxical thermic effect, maintaining an optimal room temperature, and using strategies to manage body heat, individuals can create an ideal sleep environment. These practices support the body's natural temperature fluctuations, promoting more restful and restorative sleep.

Exercise and Sleep: Finding the Balance for Optimal Rest

Exercise has a profound impact on sleep, playing a crucial role in regulating the circadian rhythm and promoting overall sleep quality. However, the timing and intensity of physical activity can significantly influence its effects on sleep.

The Impact of Exercise on Sleep

Engaging in physical activity, particularly in the morning, helps to regulate the circadian rhythm and promote wakefulness during the day. Morning exercise not only increases the rate of body temperature rise, facilitating morning wakefulness, but may also provide exposure to daylight, which further helps reset the internal clock.

Conversely, exercising too close to bedtime can interfere with sleep due to increased heart rate, metabolic rate, and core body temperature, as well as elevated levels of adrenaline. These physiological changes can make it difficult for the body to wind down and transition into a restful state.

Timing of Exercise

The timing of exercise is critical in maximizing its benefits for sleep:

Morning Exercise

- **Regulating the Circadian Rhythm**: exercising in the morning is ideal for those struggling with sleep onset. Morning workouts expose the body to natural light, helping to reset the internal clock and enhance alertness throughout the day.
- **Temperature Regulation**: morning exercise increases the rate of body temperature rise, promoting wakefulness and helping align the body's natural temperature cycle with daily activities.

Afternoon Exercise

- **Enhancing Restorative Sleep**: for those experiencing fragmented sleep, exercising in the late afternoon can be beneficial. This timing helps optimize the body's temperature cycle and supports the deep, restorative phases of sleep.
- **Avoiding Vigorous Evening Exercise**: it is generally advised to avoid vigorous exercise within four hours of bedtime. This allows the body ample time to cool down and prepare for sleep. Increased heart rate and metabolic activity close to bedtime can delay the onset of sleep and reduce sleep quality.

Pre-Bedtime Relaxation

Incorporating Relaxation Techniques

Exercise is a powerful tool for improving sleep quality, but its benefits depend heavily on the timing and type of activity. Morning exercise helps regulate the circadian rhythm and promotes wakefulness, while late afternoon workouts can enhance restorative sleep. Avoiding vigorous exercise close to bedtime and incorporating relaxation techniques can further support a healthy sleep routine. By strategically integrating exercise into your daily schedule, you can optimize your sleep and overall well-being.

Integrating COLTE into Daily Life

Integrating the principles of the COLTE mnemonic into daily routines can significantly enhance sleep quality. Here are some practical tips:

- **Carbohydrates:** Aim for a balanced, carbohydrate-rich meal approximately four hours before bedtime.
- **Osmolality:** Stay hydrated and avoid high-sodium foods, especially in the evening.
- **Light:** Get plenty of natural light exposure in the morning and minimize blue light exposure in the evening.
- **Temperature:** Maintain a comfortable room temperature for sleep and consider pre-sleep rituals that promote peripheral vasodilation, such as warm baths.
- **Exercise:** Incorporate regular exercise into the routine, preferably in the morning or late afternoon, and avoid intense workouts close to bedtime.

Conclusion

Understanding and applying the COLTE mnemonic can help health professionals and their patients achieve better sleep by addressing critical physiological and environmental factors. By optimizing carbohydrate intake, maintaining proper hydration, managing light exposure, regulating temperature, and scheduling exercise appropriately, individuals can support their natural circadian rhythms and improve overall sleep quality. Health professionals should educate patients on these factors to empower them to make informed decisions about their sleep health, ultimately enhancing their overall well-being.

Chapter 4: Insomnia and Its Management

Understanding Insomnia

Insomnia is a prevalent sleep disorder characterized by difficulty falling asleep, staying asleep, or waking up too early and being unable to fall back asleep. It affects millions of people worldwide, significantly impacting their health and quality of life. The severity of insomnia can vary, from occasional sleeplessness to chronic insomnia, which occurs at least three times a week for three months or more. The condition can lead to daytime fatigue, irritability, difficulty concentrating, and reduced performance in daily activities. Understanding insomnia involves recognizing its multifactorial aetiology, where biological, psychological, and environmental factors interplay.

Causes of Insomnia

Stress and Anxiety

One of the most common causes of insomnia is stress. Work-related stress, financial worries, and personal issues can keep the mind active, preventing relaxation and making it difficult to fall asleep. Anxiety disorders further exacerbate this problem, leading to a vicious cycle of worry and sleeplessness.

Depression

Depression is closely linked with insomnia. People with depression often experience changes in sleep patterns, including difficulty falling asleep or staying asleep. The relationship between depression and insomnia is bidirectional, meaning that each condition can exacerbate the other.

Medical Conditions

Chronic pain, asthma, gastrointestinal disorders, and neurological conditions like Parkinson's disease can interfere with sleep. Additionally, conditions such as sleep apnea and restless leg syndrome directly disrupt sleep, contributing to insomnia.

Medications

Certain medications, including those used to treat asthma, high blood pressure, and depression, can cause insomnia as a side effect. Stimulants, such as caffeine and nicotine, also contribute to difficulty in falling and staying asleep.

Lifestyle Factors

Poor sleep habits, including irregular sleep schedules, naps during the day, and engaging in stimulating activities before bedtime, can lead to insomnia. The consumption of alcohol and caffeine close to bedtime can disrupt the sleep cycle, leading to fragmented sleep.

Management of insomnia

Cognitive Behavioural Therapy for Insomnia (CBT-I)

Cognitive Behavioural Therapy for Insomnia (CBT-I) is considered the first-line treatment for chronic insomnia. It involves several techniques aimed at changing unhelpful sleep-related thoughts and behaviours, improving sleep quality, and increasing sleep efficiency.

Sleep Hygiene Education

Sleep hygiene involves educating patients about practices that promote good sleep. Key components include:

- **Maintaining a Regular Sleep Schedule**: going to bed and waking up at the same time every day, including weekends, helps regulate the body's internal clock.
- **Creating a Comfortable Sleep Environment**: ensuring the bedroom is cool, dark, and quiet can significantly improve sleep quality. Using comfortable bedding and a supportive mattress is also important.
- **Avoiding Stimulants**: caffeine and nicotine should be avoided, particularly in the afternoon and evening, as they can interfere with sleep. Limiting alcohol consumption is also advised, as it can disrupt sleep patterns.
- **Limiting Electronics**: reducing exposure to electronic devices before bedtime helps avoid blue light, which can suppress melatonin production and disrupt sleep.

Stimulus Control

Stimulus control therapy aims to associate the bed with sleep by limiting activities in bed to sleep and sex only. Key principles include:

- **Bed for Sleep Only**: using the bed only for sleep and sex helps strengthen the association between bed and sleep.
- **Go to Bed When Sleepy**: patients are advised to go to bed only when they feel sleepy.
- **Get Out of Bed If Unable to Sleep**: if unable to sleep within 20 minutes, patients should get out of bed and engage in a quiet, calming activity until they feel sleepy again. This helps prevent the bed from becoming associated with wakefulness or anxiety about not sleeping.

Cognitive Restructuring

Cognitive restructuring focuses on changing negative thoughts and beliefs about sleep. Techniques include:

- **Challenging Unrealistic Expectations**: helping patients set realistic expectations about sleep can reduce anxiety and frustration related to sleeplessness.
- **Reducing Fear of Sleeplessness**: addressing fears and anxieties about not being able to sleep can prevent these thoughts from perpetuating insomnia. Patients learn to view occasional sleeplessness as manageable and not catastrophic.

Sleep Efficiency Optimisation

Optimising sleep efficiency is a critical component of CBT-I.

- **Calculate Sleep Efficiency**: sleep efficiency is the ratio of total sleep time to time spent in bed. The goal is to achieve a sleep efficiency of at least 90-95%. To achieve a high sleep efficiency consider the following:
- **Get Up If Not Asleep Within 30 Minutes**: if unable to fall asleep within 30 minutes of going to bed, get up and engage in a quiet, calming activity such as reading or listening to soothing music until feeling sleepy.
- **Maintain a Consistent Wake-Up Time**: regardless of how much sleep was achieved during the night, it is essential to wake up at the same time every day. This consistency helps reinforce the body's sleep-wake cycle and improve overall sleep quality.
- **Gradually Increase Time in Bed**: as sleep efficiency improves, time in bed is gradually increased until the desired sleep duration is achieved without compromising sleep quality.

CBT-I offers a comprehensive approach to managing chronic insomnia through various techniques aimed at improving sleep-related thoughts and behaviours. By focusing on sleep hygiene education, stimulus control, sleep restriction, cognitive restructuring, and sleep efficiency optimization, patients can achieve better sleep quality and overall well-being.

Pharmacological Treatments

Exogenous melatonin supplementation

Melatonin, a hormone naturally produced by the pineal gland, plays a crucial role in regulating the sleep-wake cycle and circadian rhythms. Exogenous melatonin supplementation has gained popularity for its potential benefits in improving sleep quality, managing circadian rhythm disorders, and providing neuroprotective and antioxidant effects.

Pharmacodynamics and Therapeutic Effects

Melatonin has a wide range of effects on the body, influencing sleep, circadian rhythms, and various physiological processes:

Melatonin is effective in reducing sleep latency by 7-34 minutes, making it beneficial for individuals with insomnia or delayed sleep phase syndrome. While it does not significantly affect slow-wave sleep (SWS), it has a variable effect on REM sleep. Overall, melatonin increases total sleep time and sleep efficiency, contributing to improved sleep quality.

Melatonin is commonly used to manage circadian rhythm disorders such as jet lag, shift work sleep disorder, and delayed sleep phase disorder. By shifting the timing of melatonin release, it helps align the sleep-wake cycle with the desired schedule.

Melatonin can be used to help with the following clinical conditions.

Seasonal Affective Disorder (SAD):

Melatonin may alleviate symptoms of SAD by regulating circadian rhythms disrupted by reduced daylight exposure.

Alzheimer's Disease:

Melatonin's neuroprotective effects may slow cognitive decline in Alzheimer's patients by reducing oxidative stress and inflammation.

Menopause:

Melatonin supplementation may help alleviate sleep disturbances and mood changes associated with menopause.

Gastro-oesophageal Reflux Disease (GORD):

Melatonin enhances lower oesophageal sphincter (LOS) tone and suppresses gastric acid secretion, offering relief from GERD symptoms. Its antioxidant and anti-inflammatory properties further contribute to mucosal protection.

Antioxidant and Neuroprotective Effects:

Melatonin is a potent antioxidant, protecting cells from oxidative damage. This is particularly relevant in retinal health and conditions like tinnitus, where oxidative stress plays a key role in disease progression. Melatonin's ability to modulate neurotransmitter activity may also contribute to its therapeutic effects in tinnitus.

Melatonin in Special Populations

Children:

Long-term use of melatonin in children is not recommended due to insufficient safety data. Short-term use may be considered under medical supervision.

Pregnancy and Breastfeeding:

The safety of melatonin during pregnancy and breastfeeding has not been established, and its use should be avoided unless prescribed by a healthcare provider.

Older Adults:

Older adults may require lower doses of melatonin due to increased sensitivity and changes in pharmacokinetics with aging.

Pharmacokinetics of Melatonin

Melatonin is rapidly absorbed, with peak plasma concentrations achieved within 20-60 minutes of oral administration. Sublingual preparations of melatonin offer better bioavailability compared to standard oral forms, allowing for faster onset of action.

Melatonin is widely distributed throughout the body and easily crosses the blood-brain barrier (BBB). Its volume of distribution (Vd) ranges between 35 to 60 litres, indicating extensive tissue distribution.

Melatonin is primarily metabolised by the liver enzyme CYP1A2 into 6-hydroxymelatonin, which is subsequently conjugated with glucuronide or sulfate. The involvement of CYP1A2 in its metabolism highlights the potential for drug interactions with substances that induce or inhibit this enzyme.

Approximately 90% of melatonin is excreted renally as 6-sulfatoxymelatonin. The half-life of melatonin is relatively short, ranging from 30 to 60 minutes, necessitating its administration close to bedtime to be effective.

Drug-Drug Interactions

Melatonin interacts with several drugs due to its influence on cytochrome P450 (CYP) enzymes:

CYP1A2:

Melatonin is an inhibitor of CYP1A2, which is responsible for melatonin's own metabolism as well as the metabolism of drugs like caffeine and some antidepressants.

CYP2C9:

Melatonin can increase the effect of warfarin and phenytoin by inhibiting CYP2C9.

CYP2C19:

Inhibition of CYP2C19 by melatonin may affect the metabolism of omeprazole, diazepam, and clopidogrel.

No effect on CYP3A4:

Melatonin does not appear to affect CYP3A4, a major enzyme involved in drug metabolism.

Patients with diabetes should be cautious with melatonin supplementation, as it may impair glucose regulation, reduce insulin secretion, and increase insulin resistance. Additionally, melatonin can disrupt circadian rhythms, potentially exacerbating metabolic issues in diabetics.

Side Effects and Safety

Melatonin is generally well-tolerated, but it can cause side effects such as drowsiness, headache, dizziness, nausea, nightmares, mood changes, stomach cramps, and allergic reactions. Long-term use of high doses may suppress endogenous melatonin production, emphasizing the importance of using the lowest effective dose for short durations.

Dosage and Administration

Melatonin should be administered at the lowest effective dose for the shortest amount of time to minimize potential side effects. The recommended dosage is typically between 0.5 to 1 mg taken 30-60 minutes before bedtime. This timing aligns with the natural peak in melatonin levels, optimizing its efficacy in inducing sleep.

Benzodiazepines and Their Impact on Sleep

Benzodiazepines, such as temazepam and diazepam, and non-benzodiazepine hypnotics like zolpidem and eszopiclone, are sedative medications commonly prescribed to help with short-term insomnia. The effect on sleep latency varies depending on the drug in question. Diazepam reduces sleep latency by approximately 15-30 minutes; temazepam by 20-40 minutes; and zolpidem by 15-20 minutes. While these medications can be effective in inducing sleep, they carry significant risks and can negatively impact sleep architecture, making them unsuitable for long-term use.

Risks of Dependency and Tolerance
One of the primary concerns with benzodiazepines and non-benzodiazepine hypnotics is the potential for dependency and tolerance. Over time, individuals may require higher doses to achieve the same sedative effects, leading to dependency. This makes it difficult to discontinue use without experiencing withdrawal symptoms, including rebound insomnia, which can be even more severe than the initial sleep disturbance.

Effects on Sleep Architecture
Benzodiazepines and non-benzodiazepine hypnotics alter the natural stages of sleep, impacting the overall quality and restorative nature of sleep:

- **Increase in Stage 2 Non-REM Sleep**: These medications increase the amount of time spent in stage 2 non-REM sleep. While stage 2 sleep is a normal part of the sleep cycle, an overemphasis on this stage can be problematic.
- **Decrease in Stage 3 Non-REM Sleep (Slow-Wave Sleep)**: Stage 3 non-REM sleep, also known as slow-wave sleep, is crucial for physical restoration, immune function, and memory consolidation. Benzodiazepines reduce the duration of this deep, restorative sleep, which can impair these essential functions.
- **Decrease in REM Sleep**: REM sleep is vital for emotional regulation, memory processing, and cognitive function. Benzodiazepines and similar medications decrease the amount of REM sleep, potentially leading to cognitive deficits and emotional instability over time.

Short-Term Use and Monitoring

Given these effects, benzodiazepines and non-benzodiazepine hypnotics are best reserved for short-term use under careful medical supervision. They may be appropriate for managing acute insomnia or sleep disturbances due to transient stressors. However, for long-term management, alternative treatments such as Cognitive Behavioural Therapy for Insomnia (CBT-I) are preferred due to their efficacy and lower risk of adverse effects.

- **Reduction of Noradrenergic Tone**: prazosin works by blocking alpha-1 adrenergic receptors, which reduces the overall noradrenergic tone in the brain. By decreasing noradrenaline levels, prazosin helps mitigate the hyperarousal and emotional intensity that often lead to nightmares during REM sleep.
- **Improvement in REM Sleep Quality**: by modulating noradrenergic activity, prazosin helps normalize the physiological environment of REM sleep. This normalization allows for better emotional processing and a reduction in the distressing and vivid nature of nightmares.
- **Reduction in Nightmare Frequency and Severity**: clinical studies have shown that prazosin effectively reduces both the frequency and severity of nightmares in patients with PTSD. This improvement in nightmare symptoms can lead to better overall sleep quality and daytime functioning.

Clinical Implications

The use of prazosin for treating PTSD-related nightmares has significant clinical implications:

- **Enhanced Sleep Quality**: Patients often experience improved sleep quality, with fewer interruptions due to nightmares. This improvement can contribute to overall better health and well-being.
- **Daytime Functioning**: By reducing the frequency and severity of nightmares, prazosin can help alleviate daytime symptoms of PTSD, such as anxiety and hypervigilance, improving overall functioning and quality of life.
- **Emotional Stability**: Better emotional processing during REM sleep can lead to improved emotional regulation and stability, which is crucial for individuals with PTSD.

Rule of 'S' in Sleep: Drugs Affecting Slow-Wave Sleep

The quality of sleep is influenced by various factors, including the medications one takes. Certain drugs can significantly alter sleep architecture, particularly slow-wave sleep (SWS), which is crucial for restorative sleep. Understanding how different classes of medications affect sleep can help manage sleep-related issues more effectively.

Serotonergic Antidepressants (SSRIs/SNRIs)

Selective Serotonin Reuptake Inhibitors (SSRIs) and Serotonin-Norepinephrine Reuptake Inhibitors (SNRIs) are commonly prescribed to treat depression and anxiety disorders. While effective for these conditions, they can impact sleep architecture:

- **Alteration of REM and Non-REM Sleep**: SSRIs and SNRIs tend to suppress REM sleep, the phase associated with vivid dreaming and emotional processing. This suppression can lead to an imbalance in the sleep cycle, with increased time spent in lighter stages of non-REM sleep and reduced slow-wave sleep.
- **Impact on Sleep Quality**: the reduction in REM sleep and potential disturbance in SWS can affect overall sleep quality. Patients might experience more frequent awakenings and less restorative sleep, contributing to feelings of fatigue and decreased cognitive function during the day.

Stimulants

Stimulant medications, including amphetamines and cocaine, are known to have profound effects on sleep:

- **Increased Wakefulness**: stimulants are designed to increase alertness and wakefulness, often used to treat conditions like Attention Deficit Hyperactivity Disorder (ADHD) or as illicit substances. While they are effective in promoting wakefulness, they significantly reduce total sleep time.
- **Reduction in REM Sleep**: these drugs decrease the amount of REM sleep, disrupting the normal sleep cycle and leading to an overall reduction in sleep quality. The diminished REM sleep can impair cognitive functions such as memory consolidation and emotional regulation.
- **Sleep Fragmentation**: stimulants can cause sleep fragmentation, leading to frequent awakenings throughout the night and reducing the time spent in the deeper, restorative stages of sleep.

Stimulating Antidepressants (NDRIs)

Norepinephrine-Dopamine Reuptake Inhibitors (NDRIs) are another class of antidepressants that can impact sleep.

- **Reduction in Sleep Quality**: NDRIs, such as bupropion, are stimulating and can reduce overall sleep quality. These medications can increase wakefulness and make it harder for patients to fall and stay asleep.
- **Impact on Slow-Wave Sleep**: similar to other stimulating medications, NDRIs can reduce the duration of slow-wave sleep, which is essential for physical restoration and cognitive function. This reduction can lead to less restorative sleep and increased daytime fatigue.

Serotonin receptor antagonists increase SWS

Serotonin receptor antagonists have been shown to decrease sleep latency, increase slow wave sleep, and suppress REM sleep, and increase total sleep time. Examples of serotonin receptor antagonists include atypical antipsychotics, cyproheptadine, antidepressants such as mirtazapine, and anti-emetics such as ondansetron.

Alternative and Complementary Therapies

Herbal Remedies

Herbal remedies, such as valerian root, chamomile, and lavender, have been used traditionally to promote sleep. While some studies suggest benefits, more research is needed to confirm their efficacy and safety.

Acupuncture

Acupuncture, a traditional Chinese medicine practice, involves inserting thin needles into specific points on the body. Some studies suggest it may help improve sleep quality, though the evidence is not conclusive.

Relaxation Techniques

Relaxation techniques, including deep breathing, progressive muscle relaxation, and guided imagery, can help reduce stress and anxiety, promoting better sleep. Incorporating these techniques into a bedtime routine can be beneficial.

The Role of Technology in Insomnia Management

In the modern era, technology plays a significant role in managing insomnia, offering innovative solutions to monitor, diagnose, and treat sleep disorders. From sleep tracking devices to telemedicine and wearable technology designed to stimulate sleep, these tools provide valuable insights and accessibility for better sleep management.

Sleep Tracking Devices

Wearable sleep trackers and smartphone apps have revolutionized the way we understand and monitor our sleep patterns. These devices can track various aspects of sleep, including duration, quality, and different sleep stages (light, deep, and REM sleep). The data collected from these devices can help identify sleep issues and monitor improvements over time, offering a personalized approach to sleep management.

- **Monitoring Sleep Patterns**: devices such as the Fitbit, Apple Watch, and Oura Ring provide detailed reports on sleep cycles, heart rate, and movements during sleep. This information can be crucial for identifying patterns and disruptions in sleep.
- **Identifying Sleep Issues**: by analyzing the data, users and healthcare providers can pinpoint specific issues such as frequent awakenings, insufficient deep sleep, or irregular sleep schedules.
- **Tracking Progress**: continuous monitoring allows for the assessment of how changes in lifestyle, medication, or therapy affect sleep quality, helping to refine and improve treatment plans.

Wearable Technology for Sleep Stimulation

Beyond tracking, some wearable technologies are designed to actively improve sleep quality by stimulating sleep through various means.

- **Sleep Headbands**: devices like the "Dreem headband" use EEG technology to monitor brain activity and provide auditory stimulation to enhance deep sleep. By playing specific sounds during slow-wave sleep, these headbands aim to increase the duration and quality of deep sleep.
- **Smart Mattresses and Pillows**: products like the Eight Sleep Pod Pro use temperature regulation and gentle vibrations to help users fall asleep faster and stay asleep longer. These smart mattresses can adjust their temperature based on the user's sleep cycle, promoting better sleep quality.
- **Wearable Electrotherapy Devices**: devices such as the Fisher Wallace Stimulator deliver gentle electrical currents to the brain to promote relaxation and improve sleep. These wearable devices aim to reduce insomnia symptoms by enhancing the production of serotonin and melatonin while reducing cortisol levels.

Telemedicine

Telemedicine has emerged as a powerful tool in the management of insomnia, offering remote diagnosis and treatment options. This approach increases access to care for individuals in remote or underserved areas, providing a convenient and effective way to address sleep disorders.

- **Remote Diagnosis and Treatment**: virtual consultations with sleep specialists allow for thorough assessments and personalized treatment plans without the need for in-person visits. This is particularly beneficial for those who have difficulty accessing traditional healthcare services.
- **Ongoing Support**: telemedicine platforms can provide continuous support and follow-up appointments, ensuring that patients receive the necessary adjustments to their treatment plans. This ongoing care is crucial for managing chronic insomnia effectively.

Lifestyle Modifications

Regular Physical Activity

Balanced Diet

Engaging in regular physical activity can improve sleep quality and duration. However, it is important to avoid vigorous exercise close to bedtime as it can be stimulating.

A balanced diet that avoids heavy, spicy, or sugary foods before bedtime can promote better sleep. Maintaining a healthy weight can also reduce the risk of sleep apnea, which is often associated with insomnia.

Stress Management

Effective stress management techniques, such as mindfulness meditation, yoga, and cognitive behavioral strategies, can help reduce anxiety and improve sleep.

Dark Therapy for Mania

Dark Therapy

Reducing exposure to artificial light, particularly blue light, in the evening can help stabilize mood and improve sleep quality in individuals with bipolar disorder. This therapy involves spending time in a dark environment to promote melatonin production and regulate the sleep-wake cycle.

Conclusion

Insomnia is a complex condition with multiple causes and significant impacts on health and quality of life. Effective management requires a comprehensive approach that includes behavioral therapies, pharmacological treatments, and lifestyle modifications. Health professionals play a crucial role in identifying the underlying causes of insomnia and providing tailored treatment plans to help patients achieve better sleep. By integrating traditional and complementary therapies, promoting good sleep hygiene, and leveraging technology, we can significantly improve the management of insomnia and enhance overall well-being.

Chapter 5: Sleep Apnea and Other Sleep-Related Breathing Disorders

Understanding Sleep Apnea

Sleep apnea is a serious sleep disorder characterized by repeated interruptions in breathing during sleep. These interruptions, known as apneas, can last from a few seconds to minutes, typically ranging from 10 to 30 seconds, and occur multiple times throughout the night. These interruptions disrupt sleep and reduce oxygen levels in the blood, leading to various health complications. There are two main types of sleep apnea:

Types of Sleep Apnea
Obstructive Sleep Apnea (OSA)

- **Mechanism**: OSA is the most common form of sleep apnea. It occurs when the muscles in the back of the throat relax excessively, causing a temporary blockage of the airway. This obstruction leads to interrupted breathing.
- **Symptoms**: common symptoms of OSA include loud snoring, gasping or choking during sleep, frequent awakenings, and excessive daytime sleepiness. Individuals with OSA may also experience headaches, difficulty concentrating, and mood changes.
- **Risk Factors**: risk factors for OSA include obesity, large neck circumference, narrow airway, being male, older age, family history, use of alcohol or sedatives, and smoking.

Central Sleep Apnea (CSA)

- **Mechanism**: CSA occurs when the brain fails to send proper signals to the muscles that control breathing. Unlike OSA, the airway is not blocked, but the brain fails to initiate a breath.
- **Symptoms**: symptoms of CSA can overlap with those of OSA and include pauses in breathing, abrupt awakenings with shortness of breath, and excessive daytime sleepiness. CSA is less common than OSA.
- **Risk Factors**: risk factors for CSA include heart disorders, stroke, brainstem injury or disease, opioid use, and high altitudes.

Health Implications

Sleep apnea can have serious health consequences if left untreated. The repeated interruptions in breathing and subsequent drops in oxygen levels can lead to:

- **Cardiovascular Problems**: sleep apnea increases the risk of high blood pressure, heart attack, stroke, and irregular heartbeats.
- **Diabetes**: there is a strong link between sleep apnea and insulin resistance, which can contribute to type 2 diabetes.
- **Daytime Fatigue**: the frequent awakenings prevent restorative sleep, leading to severe daytime drowsiness, fatigue, and irritability. This can affect concentration and increase the risk of accidents.
- **Metabolic Syndrome**: this cluster of conditions includes high blood pressure, abnormal cholesterol levels, high blood sugar, and increased waist circumference, all of which are linked to sleep apnea.

Diagnosis and Screening

Screening Tools

Screening tools, such as the STOP-Bang questionnaire, can help identify individuals at risk for sleep apnea. The STOP-Bang questionnaire includes questions about snoring, tiredness, observed apneas, high blood pressure, body mass index (BMI), age, neck circumference, and gender. A higher score indicates a greater risk of sleep apnea and the need for further evaluation.

The STOP-Bang Questionnaire is available on the following link

http://www.stopbang.ca/osa/screening.php

Polysomnography (Sleep Study)

Polysomnography is the gold standard for diagnosing sleep apnea. It involves an overnight stay in a sleep lab, where various physiological parameters are monitored, including brain activity, eye movements, muscle activity, heart rate, respiratory effort, airflow, and blood oxygen levels. This comprehensive assessment helps identify the presence and severity of sleep apnea.

Home Sleep Apnea Testing

Home sleep apnea testing (HSAT) is a more convenient and cost-effective option for diagnosing OSA. HSAT involves using portable monitoring devices at home to record similar parameters as polysomnography, although it may not be as comprehensive. HSAT is suitable for patients with a high likelihood of moderate to severe OSA and without significant comorbidities.

Managing Sleep-Related Breathing Disorders

Addressing Underlying Conditions

Managing underlying conditions that contribute to sleep-related breathing disorders is crucial. Conditions such as heart failure, hypothyroidism, and nasal congestion should be treated to improve overall respiratory function and reduce apneas.

Lifestyle Changes

Lifestyle changes can help manage and reduce the severity of OSA. These changes include:

- **Weight Loss:** Losing weight can reduce the amount of fat around the neck and throat, decreasing airway obstruction.
- **Avoiding Alcohol and Sedatives:** Alcohol and sedatives relax the muscles of the throat, increasing the risk of airway collapse.
- **Sleeping on the Side:** Sleeping on the back can cause the tongue and soft tissues to obstruct the airway. Positional therapy, such as using special pillows or devices, can help maintain a side-sleeping position.

Positional Therapy

- Positional therapy involves techniques to prevent sleeping on the back, which can worsen OSA. Devices such as positional pillows or vibrating alarms can help patients maintain a side-sleeping position throughout the night.
- **Tennis Ball Technique:** a simple and effective positional therapy for sleep apnea involves sewing a tennis ball into the back of pyjamas. This discourages patients from sleeping on their backs, a position that can exacerbate sleep apnea symptoms.

Oral Appliances

Oral appliances, also known as mandibular advancement devices (MADs), are custom-made devices worn in the mouth during sleep. They work by repositioning the lower jaw and tongue to keep the airway open. Oral appliances are suitable for patients with mild to moderate OSA who cannot tolerate CPAP therapy or prefer an alternative treatment.

Supplemental Oxygen

Supplemental oxygen may be prescribed for patients with CSA or those with significant oxygen desaturation during sleep. Oxygen therapy can help maintain adequate blood oxygen levels and reduce symptoms.

Continuous Positive Airway Pressure (CPAP) Therapy and Alternatives

Continuous Positive Airway Pressure (CPAP) therapy is widely regarded as the most effective treatment for Obstructive Sleep Apnea (OSA). This therapy, along with its alternatives like Automatic Positive Airway Pressure (APAP) and Adaptive Servo-Ventilation (ASV), plays a crucial role in managing sleep apnea by ensuring the airway remains open during sleep, thereby improving sleep quality and reducing associated health risks.

CPAP (Continuous Positive Airway Pressure)

CPAP therapy involves wearing a mask connected to a machine that delivers a constant stream of air, keeping the airway open during sleep. This steady air pressure prevents airway collapse, significantly reducing apneas and improving sleep quality.

- **Mechanism**: A CPAP machine provides a continuous, fixed pressure of air through a mask that covers the nose and/or mouth.
- **Effectiveness**: CPAP is highly effective in preventing airway obstruction during sleep, reducing the risk of associated health problems such as hypertension and cardiovascular disease.
- **Benefits**: Improved sleep quality, reduced daytime fatigue, and decreased risk of cardiovascular complications are primary benefits of CPAP therapy.

APAP (Automatic Positive Airway Pressure)

APAP devices offer a more flexible alternative to CPAP by automatically adjusting the pressure throughout the night based on the patient's needs.

- **Mechanism**: APAP machines continuously monitor breathing and adjust the air pressure accordingly. They provide higher pressure when needed (e.g., during REM sleep or when lying on the back) and lower pressure when less support is required.
- **Benefits**: APAP is particularly beneficial for patients who have varying pressure needs during the night or those who find it difficult to tolerate a fixed pressure setting. This adaptability can enhance comfort and compliance with therapy.

Comparing CPAP and APAP

- **CPAP**: Delivers a constant, fixed pressure; effective in preventing airway collapse; commonly used for treating OSA.
- **APAP**: Adjusts pressure automatically based on the patient's breathing patterns; beneficial for variable pressure needs and improved comfort.

ASV (Adaptive Servo-Ventilation)

ASV is specifically designed to treat Central Sleep Apnea (CSA), a condition where the brain fails to send proper signals to the muscles that control breathing.

- **Mechanism**: ASV devices monitor breathing and deliver variable pressure support to maintain stable breathing patterns. They adjust the pressure support dynamically to normalize breathing and reduce apneas.
- **Effectiveness**: ASV is particularly effective for patients with CSA, as it can respond to the unique needs of these patients by providing just the right amount of pressure support.
- **Benefits**: By stabilizing breathing patterns, ASV helps improve sleep quality and reduce the symptoms associated with CSA, such as excessive daytime sleepiness and cardiovascular issues.

Surgical Options

Surgical options may be considered for severe OSA or when other treatments are ineffective. These procedures include:

- **Uvulopalatopharyngoplasty (UPPP)**: removal of excess tissue from the throat to widen the airway.
- **Genioglossus Advancement (GA)**: repositioning the tongue muscle attachment to prevent airway collapse.
- **Maxillomandibular Advancement (MMA)**: repositioning the upper and lower jaw to enlarge the airway.

The Role of Technology in Sleep Apnea Management

Wearable Devices

Wearable devices, such as smartwatches and fitness trackers, can monitor sleep patterns and detect potential sleep apnea episodes. These devices provide valuable data that can help patients and healthcare providers track progress and adjust treatment plans.

Telemedicine

Telemedicine offers remote diagnosis and management of sleep apnea. Virtual consultations with sleep specialists can provide personalized treatment plans, follow-up care, and ongoing support, increasing access to care for individuals in remote or underserved areas.

Patient Education and Support

Understanding Treatment Options

Educating patients about the various treatment options and their benefits is essential for adherence and successful management of sleep apnea. Patients should be informed about the importance of CPAP therapy, the use of oral appliances, and the potential need for surgical interventions.

Lifestyle Modifications

Encouraging patients to make lifestyle modifications, such as weight loss, avoiding alcohol, and improving sleep hygiene, can significantly enhance treatment outcomes. Support groups and resources can provide additional guidance and motivation.

Conclusion

Sleep apnea and other sleep-related breathing disorders are serious conditions that require comprehensive management. Accurate diagnosis through polysomnography or home sleep apnea testing, followed by appropriate treatment, can significantly improve sleep quality and reduce associated health risks. Health professionals play a crucial role in educating patients, providing personalized treatment plans, and offering ongoing support to ensure successful management of these disorders. By integrating lifestyle changes, technological advancements, and a multidisciplinary approach, we can improve outcomes for individuals with sleep-related breathing disorders.

Chapter 6: The Role of Technology in Sleep Management

Sleep Tracking Devices

Sleep tracking devices have revolutionized the way individuals monitor and manage their sleep health. These devices range from wearable technologies to smartphone apps, smart mattresses, and plllows, each offering unique features to provide comprehensive insights into sleep patterns and quality.

Wearable Devices

Wearable sleep tracking devices, such as smartwatches and fitness trackers, have become increasingly popular for monitoring sleep patterns. These devices use sensors to measure movement, heart rate, and sometimes even blood oxygen levels to provide insights into sleep duration, quality, and stages. Wearable devices can help individuals identify sleep issues, track improvements over time, and make informed decisions about their sleep habits.

- **Smartwatches and Fitness Trackers**: popular devices like the Apple Watch, Fitbit, and Garmin watches offer sleep tracking capabilities. These wearables monitor various physiological parameters, including heart rate variability, respiratory rate, and skin temperature, providing a comprehensive understanding of sleep health.
- **Wearable Sleep Monitors**: advanced wearable sleep monitors go beyond basic tracking. They measure detailed physiological parameters, such as heart rate variability, respiratory rate, and skin temperature. These features provide deeper insights into sleep health and can help identify underlying health issues.

Wearable Sleep Induction Technology

Innovations in wearable technology have introduced devices designed to not only track but also improve sleep quality through sleep induction techniques.

- **Sleep Headbands**: devices like the Dreem headband use EEG technology to monitor brain activity and provide auditory stimulation to enhance deep sleep. These headbands play specific sounds during slow-wave sleep to increase its duration and quality.
- **Wearable Electrotherapy Devices**: devices such as the Fisher Wallace Stimulator deliver gentle electrical currents to the brain, promoting relaxation and improving sleep. These wearables enhance the production of serotonin and melatonin while reducing cortisol levels.

Smartphone Apps

Smartphone apps can also track sleep by using the phone's accelerometer and microphone to detect movement and sounds during sleep. These apps provide detailed reports on sleep patterns, including time spent in different sleep stages, sleep efficiency, and the number of awakenings. Some apps offer additional features, such as sleep coaching, relaxation exercises, and personalized recommendations to improve sleep quality.

Popular Apps

Smart Mattresses and Pillows

Smart mattresses and pillows are equipped with sensors that monitor sleep position, movement, heart rate, and breathing patterns. These devices provide comprehensive sleep data and can adjust firmness, temperature, and support to enhance comfort and improve sleep quality. Some smart mattresses can also integrate with smart home systems to create a sleep-friendly environment by controlling lighting, temperature, and sound.

- **Smart Mattresses**: products like the Eight Sleep Pod Pro use temperature regulation and gentle vibrations to help users fall asleep faster and stay asleep longer. These mattresses adjust their temperature based on the user's sleep cycle.
- **Smart Pillows**: pillows with built-in sensors can track head position, breathing patterns, and snoring. Some can adjust their firmness to reduce snoring or improve comfort.

Sleep tracking devices, from wearables and smartphone apps to smart mattresses and pillows, offer valuable tools for monitoring and improving sleep health. By providing detailed insights into sleep patterns and quality, these technologies help individuals make informed decisions about their sleep habits and identify potential health issues. Innovations in wearable sleep induction technology further enhance the potential for achieving better, more restorative sleep.

Telemedicine and Sleep Disorders

Remote Diagnosis and Treatment

Telemedicine has revolutionised the diagnosis and treatment of sleep disorders by providing remote access to sleep specialists. Virtual consultations allow patients to receive expert advice, personalised treatment plans, and ongoing support without the need for in-person visits. This approach is particularly beneficial for individuals in remote or underserved areas, where access to sleep clinics may be limited.

Home Sleep Apnea Testing

Home sleep apnea testing (HSAT) is a convenient and cost-effective alternative to in-lab polysomnography for diagnosing obstructive sleep apnea (OSA). HSAT devices are sent to the patient's home, where they are used to monitor breathing patterns, oxygen levels, and heart rate during sleep. The data is then analysed remotely by sleep specialists, who provide a diagnosis and recommend appropriate treatment.

Telehealth Platforms

Telehealth platforms offer comprehensive solutions for managing sleep disorders, including scheduling virtual appointments, accessing medical records, and receiving follow-up care. These platforms can also provide educational resources, sleep hygiene tips, and support groups to help patients manage their sleep health effectively.

The Impact of Blue Light and Screen Time

Blue Light and Melatonin Suppression

Exposure to blue light from screens, such as smartphones, tablets, and computers, can disrupt sleep by suppressing melatonin production. Melatonin is a hormone that regulates the sleep-wake cycle, and its suppression can delay sleep onset and reduce sleep quality. Blue light exposure in the evening can lead to difficulty falling asleep, shorter sleep duration, and poorer sleep quality.

Strategies to Mitigate Blue Light Exposure

To mitigate the impact of blue light on sleep, individuals can:

- **Use Blue Light Filters**: many devices offer built-in blue light filters or "night mode" settings that reduce blue light emission. Additionally, blue light blocking glasses can be worn in the evening.
- **Reduce Screen Time Before Bed**: limiting screen time at least one hour before bedtime can help minimise blue light exposure and promote better sleep.
- **Create a Screen-Free Bedroom**: keeping electronic devices out of the bedroom can reduce the temptation to use screens before bed and create a more conducive sleep environment.

Light Therapy: Regulating Circadian Rhythms and Improving Sleep Quality

Light therapy is an effective treatment for regulating the circadian rhythm and enhancing sleep quality. By using light therapy devices such as light boxes and dawn simulators, individuals can mimic natural sunlight exposure, which is crucial for maintaining a healthy sleep-wake cycle.

The Mechanism of Light Therapy

Light therapy works by exposing individuals to bright light that simulates natural daylight. This exposure helps reset the internal biological clock, known as the circadian rhythm, which governs sleep-wake cycles and other physiological processes. Regular exposure to bright light in the morning can help align the circadian rhythm with the external environment, making it easier to fall asleep at night and wake up in the morning.

Types of Light Therapy Devices

Light Boxes

- **Potency**: light boxes typically emit light at an intensity of 10,000 lux, which is significantly brighter than standard indoor lighting but less intense than direct sunlight. This high-intensity light is crucial for effectively resetting the circadian rhythm.
- **Usage**: to use a light box, individuals should sit in front of the device for about 20 to 30 minutes each morning. The light should enter the eyes indirectly, so it's important not to stare directly at the light source.
- **Considerations**: light boxes are especially useful for people living in areas with reduced natural sunlight, such as northern Scandinavia during the winter months. They provide a reliable alternative to natural sunlight, helping to prevent seasonal affective disorder (SAD) and other circadian rhythm-related sleep issues.

Dawn Simulators

- **Function**: dawn simulators gradually increase the light intensity in the bedroom, mimicking a natural sunrise. This gradual increase in light helps to gently wake individuals, aligning their internal clock with the external environment.
- **Benefits**: dawn simulators are particularly beneficial for individuals who have difficulty waking up in the morning. They provide a more natural and less jarring wake-up experience compared to traditional alarm clocks.

The Benefits of Natural Light
While light therapy devices are effective, natural sunlight remains the most potent and beneficial light source for regulating circadian rhythms.

- **Sky Gazing**: spending time outdoors and sky gazing can provide exposure to natural light, which is more effective than artificial light in regulating the circadian rhythm. Even on cloudy days, outdoor light is significantly brighter and more beneficial than indoor lighting.
- **Daily Outdoor Exposure**: aim for at least 30 minutes of outdoor light exposure each day, especially in the morning. Activities such as walking, jogging, or simply sitting outside can help maintain a healthy circadian rhythm and improve sleep quality.

Light Therapy in Specific Conditions

- **Seasonal Affective Disorder (SAD)**: light therapy is a well-established treatment for SAD, a type of depression that occurs during the winter months when natural sunlight is limited. Light boxes can help alleviate the symptoms of SAD by compensating for the lack of natural light.
- **Shift Work and Jet Lag**: for individuals with irregular work schedules or those experiencing jet lag, light therapy can help adjust the circadian rhythm to the desired schedule, reducing the impact of sleep disruptions.

The Role of Artificial Intelligence in Sleep Management

AI-Powered Sleep Analysis

Artificial intelligence (AI) is transforming sleep management by providing advanced analysis of sleep data. AI algorithms can process large amounts of sleep data collected from wearable devices, smart mattresses, and sleep apps to identify patterns and detect sleep disorders. AI-powered sleep analysis can offer personalised insights and recommendations to improve sleep quality.

Predictive Analytics

Predictive analytics uses historical sleep data to forecast future sleep patterns and potential issues. By identifying trends and anomalies, predictive analytics can help individuals and healthcare providers take proactive measures to prevent sleep problems and optimise sleep health.

AI-Driven Sleep Coaching

AI-driven sleep coaching platforms use machine learning algorithms to provide personalised sleep recommendations based on individual sleep data and preferences. These platforms can offer tailored advice on sleep hygiene, bedtime routines, and lifestyle changes to enhance sleep quality.

Innovations in Sleep Technology

Sleep Environment Optimisation

Smart home technology can create an optimal sleep environment by controlling lighting, temperature, and sound. Smart lighting systems can simulate natural sunrise and sunset, while smart thermostats can maintain a comfortable room temperature throughout the night. White noise machines and sleep soundscapes can mask disruptive noises and promote relaxation.

Virtual Reality for Relaxation

Virtual reality (VR) technology is being explored as a tool for relaxation and stress reduction before bedtime. VR relaxation programs can provide immersive experiences, such as guided meditations, calming nature scenes, and breathing exercises, to help individuals unwind and prepare for sleep.

Conclusion

Technology plays a pivotal role in modern sleep management, offering innovative solutions to monitor, diagnose, and treat sleep disorders. Wearable devices, smartphone apps, and smart home technology provide valuable insights into sleep patterns and help create a conducive sleep environment. Telemedicine and AI-powered tools enhance access to care and personalised treatment plans, while strategies to mitigate blue light exposure and optimise the sleep environment promote better sleep quality. By embracing these technological advancements, health professionals and individuals can work together to improve sleep health and overall well-being.

Chapter 7: Pediatric Sleep

The Impact of Sleep on Child Development

Cognitive Development

Adequate sleep is essential for cognitive development in children. It supports memory consolidation, learning, and problem-solving skills. Poor sleep can lead to difficulties with attention, concentration, and academic performance.

Behaviour Regulation

Physical Health

Sleep plays a crucial role in regulating emotions and behaviour. Children who do not get enough sleep may exhibit irritability, hyperactivity, and difficulty managing emotions. Consistent sleep patterns can help improve mood and behaviour.

Sleep is vital for physical growth and development. Growth hormone is primarily released during deep sleep, and adequate sleep supports immune function and overall health. Chronic sleep deprivation can increase the risk of obesity, diabetes, and other health issues.

Social and Emotional Well-Being

Good sleep is associated with better social interactions and emotional well-being. Children who sleep well are more likely to engage positively with peers and family members and have better emotional regulation.

Sleep Needs Across Childhood

Infants (0-12 Months)

Infants require significant amounts of sleep, typically ranging from 14 to 17 hours per day. Newborns may sleep in short bursts throughout the day and night, gradually consolidating sleep into longer stretches as they grow. Establishing a consistent sleep routine, including regular nap times and bedtime, can help infants develop healthy sleep patterns.

Toddlers (1-3 Years)

Toddlers need about 11 to 14 hours of sleep per day, including naps. Consistent bedtime routines, such as reading a story or singing a lullaby, can help signal that it is time for sleep. Toddlers may experience sleep disruptions due to developmental milestones, separation anxiety, or nightmares.

Preschoolers (3-5 Years)

Preschoolers typically require 10 to 13 hours of sleep per day. Establishing a consistent sleep schedule and a calming bedtime routine can help preschoolers transition to sleep more easily. Limiting screen time and avoiding stimulating activities before bed are important for promoting good sleep.

School-Age Children (6-12 Years)

School-age children need about 9 to 12 hours of sleep per night. As children begin school, maintaining a regular sleep schedule becomes crucial for their academic performance and overall health. Encouraging a relaxing bedtime routine and creating a sleep-friendly environment can support healthy sleep habits.

Teenagers (13-18 Years)

Teenagers require 8 to 10 hours of sleep per night. However, hormonal changes and increased academic and social demands can lead to irregular sleep patterns and sleep deprivation.

Common Paediatric Sleep Disorders

Night Terrors

Night terrors are episodes of intense fear, screaming, and thrashing during sleep, typically occurring in the first few hours of the night. Unlike nightmares, children experiencing night terrors are not fully awake and usually do not remember the episodes. Night terrors can be distressing for both the child and the parents, but they often resolve on their own with time.

Sleepwalking

Sleepwalking involves walking or performing other activities while still asleep. It usually occurs during deep sleep and can be triggered by factors such as sleep deprivation, illness, or stress. Ensuring a safe sleep environment and maintaining a consistent sleep schedule can help reduce the frequency of sleepwalking episodes.

Restless Leg Syndrome (RLS)

RLS is a condition characterised by an irresistible urge to move the legs, often accompanied by uncomfortable sensations. It can interfere with a child's ability to fall asleep and stay asleep. Addressing underlying causes, such as iron deficiency, and implementing lifestyle changes, such as regular exercise and good sleep hygiene, can help manage RLS symptoms.

Obstructive Sleep Apnea (OSA)

OSA in children is characterised by repeated interruptions in breathing during sleep due to airway obstruction. Symptoms include loud snoring, gasping for air, and restless sleep. OSA can affect growth, behaviour, and cognitive development. Treatment options may include adenotonsillectomy (removal of tonsils and adenoids), continuous positive airway pressure (CPAP) therapy, and lifestyle changes.

Delayed sleep phase disorder

Delayed Sleep Phase Disorder (DSPD) is a circadian rhythm sleep disorder where an individual's sleep-wake cycle is delayed by two or more hours relative to societal norms, making it difficult to fall asleep and wake up at conventional times. This condition is especially prevalent among teenagers typically between the ages of 13 to 19 years. The disorder's prevalence in teenagers is linked to biological changes during puberty that shift the sleep-wake cycle naturally later, in combination with psychosocial factors such as academic demands and increased use of electronic devices.

Strategies for Improving Pediatric Sleep

Establishing Consistent Bedtime Routines

Creating a consistent bedtime routine helps signal to children that it is time for sleep. Activities such as taking a warm bath, reading a book, or listening to calming music can promote relaxation and make the transition to sleep easier.

Creating a Sleep-Conducive Environment

A sleep-friendly environment includes a comfortable mattress, appropriate bedding, and a cool, dark, and quiet room. Using blackout curtains, white noise machines, and maintaining a comfortable room temperature can enhance sleep quality.

Managing Screen Time

Limiting screen time before bed is crucial for promoting good sleep. The blue light emitted by screens can interfere with melatonin production, making it harder for children to fall asleep. Encouraging screen-free activities in the evening can help create a more conducive environment for sleep.

Encouraging Physical Activity

Regular physical activity can help children expend energy and promote better sleep. However, it is important to avoid vigorous exercise close to bedtime, as it can be stimulating and interfere with sleep.

Management of delayed sleep phase disorder in teenagers

Management of DSPD in teenagers typically involves a combination of behavioral and pharmacological approaches, which may include:

Chronotherapy

This involves gradually advancing the teenager's sleep time by 15-30 minutes each day until the desired sleep-wake schedule is achieved.

Light Therapy

Exposure to bright light in the morning can help advance the sleep-wake cycle. Conversely, limiting exposure to bright light, especially blue light, in the evening can prevent further delay.

Melatonin Supplementation

Administering low doses of melatonin in the early evening can help realign the sleep-wake cycle by signaling the body to prepare for sleep earlier.

Sleep Hygiene Education

Encouraging consistent sleep and wake times, minimising caffeine intake, and creating a relaxing pre-sleep routine are essential.

Conclusion

Pediatric sleep is a critical component of overall health and development. Understanding the unique sleep needs of children at different stages and implementing strategies to promote good sleep hygiene can significantly enhance their well-being. By addressing common sleep disorders, establishing consistent routines, and creating a sleep-conducive environment, health professionals and parents can help children achieve the restorative sleep they need for optimal growth, learning, and emotional health. Promoting good sleep habits from an early age sets the foundation for lifelong healthy sleep patterns and overall well-being.

Chapter 8: Sleep and Mental Health

The Impact of Sleep on Overall Mental Health

Adequate sleep is essential for maintaining overall mental health. It plays a critical role in emotional regulation, cognitive function, and stress resilience. Chronic sleep disturbances can significantly impair these functions and increase the risk of developing mental health disorders.

Emotional Regulation

Sleep is vital for emotional regulation, helping individuals manage their emotions effectively.

- **Mood Stability**: adequate sleep contributes to mood stability, reducing the likelihood of irritability and mood swings. Poor sleep, on the other hand, can lead to increased irritability and difficulty managing emotions.
- **Risk of Mood Disorders**: chronic sleep deprivation is linked to a higher risk of developing mood disorders such as depression and anxiety. This connection underscores the importance of good sleep hygiene and interventions to improve sleep quality in those experiencing mood disturbances.

Cognitive Function

Sleep is crucial for various aspects of cognitive function, impacting daily activities and quality of life.

- **Memory Consolidation**: during sleep, especially during slow-wave sleep (SWS) and REM sleep, the brain processes and consolidates memories. Poor sleep can disrupt this process, leading to difficulties in learning and memory retention.
- **Attention and Decision-Making**: adequate sleep enhances attention, problem-solving, and decision-making abilities. Sleep disturbances can impair cognitive performance, leading to difficulties in daily functioning, work, and personal life.
- **Sleep and Cognitive Health**: as highlighted earlier, medications such as benzodiazepines and non-benzodiazepine hypnotics can alter sleep architecture by reducing REM and slow-wave sleep, which are crucial for cognitive function. Understanding and managing the impact of these medications is essential for maintaining cognitive health.

Stress Resilience

Good sleep enhances the body's ability to cope with stress, contributing to overall mental resilience.

- **Coping Mechanisms**: quality sleep helps the body and mind recover from daily stressors, enhancing the ability to manage challenges effectively. Sleep deprivation can lower stress resilience, making it harder to cope with daily pressures and increasing the risk of mental health issues.
- **Impact on Mental Health**: chronic sleep deprivation can exacerbate stress and lead to a vicious cycle of poor sleep and increased stress, further impacting mental health. Interventions that improve sleep quality can break this cycle, promoting better stress management and mental well-being.

The Bidirectional Relationship Between Sleep and Mental Health

Sleep and mental health are intimately connected, with each influencing the other in a bidirectional relationship. Poor sleep can contribute to the development and exacerbation of mental health disorders, while mental health conditions can lead to sleep disturbances. Understanding this complex interplay is crucial for effective treatment and management of both sleep and mental health issues.

Sleep in Mood Disorders and Anxiety

Sleep disturbances are common in mood disorders and anxiety, significantly impacting overall health and well-being. Addressing sleep issues in these conditions is crucial, as poor sleep can exacerbate symptoms and hinder recovery. Below, we explore how sleep is affected in depression, mania, and anxiety, and the interventions that can help improve both sleep and mood.

Depression

Depression is often associated with sleep disturbances, which can manifest as either insomnia or hypersomnia.

- **Insomnia**: insomnia in depression typically involves difficulty falling asleep, frequent awakenings throughout the night, and early morning awakenings. These disruptions can lead to inadequate sleep, worsening depressive symptoms and making recovery more challenging.
- **Hypersomnia**: on the other hand, some individuals with depression may experience hypersomnia, characterized by prolonged nighttime sleep or excessive daytime sleepiness. Despite spending more time in bed, the quality of sleep may still be poor.
- **Light Therapy**: light therapy can be an effective intervention for those experiencing insomnia related to depression. Exposure to bright light in the morning can help reset the circadian rhythm, making it easier to fall asleep at night and wake up in the morning. This can improve sleep quality and alleviate depressive symptoms.

- **Interventions**: cognitive Behavioral Therapy for Insomnia (CBT-I) and other sleep-focused interventions can be effective in improving both sleep and mood. CBT-I helps by modifying unhelpful thoughts and behaviors related to sleep, promoting healthier sleep patterns.

Mania

Mania, a state associated with bipolar disorder, significantly affects sleep.

- **Reduced Need for Sleep**: individuals experiencing mania often have a reduced need for sleep. They may feel energetic and require very little sleep without feeling tired, which can further exacerbate manic symptoms.
- **Sleep Disruption and Manic Episodes**: sleep disruption can trigger manic episodes, and conversely, manic episodes can cause insomnia. The lack of sleep can lead to increased impulsivity, poor judgment, and heightened irritability.
- **Dark Therapy**: to help manage mania, dark therapy can be beneficial. This involves reducing exposure to light in the evening and night to help stabilize the circadian rhythm. Using blackout curtains and minimizing screen time before bed can promote better sleep.

- **Interventions**: managing sleep in individuals with bipolar disorder involves maintaining a regular sleep schedule and addressing any sleep disruptions promptly. Medications that stabilize mood and regulate sleep, along with CBT-I, can help manage these symptoms effectively.

Anxiety

Anxiety disorders frequently cause sleep disturbances, particularly insomnia.

- **Difficulty Falling Asleep**: people with anxiety often have trouble falling asleep due to excessive worry and rumination. Their minds may race with anxious thoughts, making it hard to relax and drift off to sleep.
- **Physical Symptoms**: anxiety can also cause physical symptoms such as increased heart rate and muscle tension, which further interfere with the ability to fall and stay asleep.
- **Interventions**: treating anxiety often involves a combination of Cognitive Behavioral Therapy (CBT), medication, and relaxation techniques. Improving sleep hygiene and addressing sleep-specific issues through CBT-I can help reduce anxiety symptoms and enhance overall sleep quality.

Key Differences in Sleep Patterns

- **Depression**: individuals with depression often feel a strong need to sleep but have a reduced ability to do so effectively. Insomnia is common, and even when sleep is achieved, it may not be restorative.
- **Mania**: in contrast, those experiencing mania have a reduced need for sleep. They may sleep very little but still feel energetic, which can perpetuate the manic state.
- **Anxiety**: people with anxiety may struggle with falling asleep and staying asleep due to persistent worry and physical symptoms, leading to fragmented and insufficient sleep.

Sleep and PTSD

Nightmares and Insomnia

Post-traumatic stress disorder (PTSD) often involves significant sleep disturbances, including nightmares and insomnia. Nightmares related to traumatic events can cause frequent awakenings and contribute to a fear of sleeping. Insomnia in PTSD may involve difficulty falling asleep, staying asleep, or experiencing non-restorative sleep.

Trauma-Focused Therapies

Treating sleep disturbances in PTSD often requires a combination of trauma-focused therapies, such as prolonged exposure therapy or cognitive processing therapy, and sleep-specific interventions. Techniques like imagery rehearsal therapy can help reduce the frequency and intensity of nightmares by encouraging patients to re-script their nightmares with more positive endings.

Medication

Medications, such as prazosin, can be used to reduce the frequency and severity of nightmares in PTSD. Antidepressants and anxiolytics may also be prescribed to address underlying mental health symptoms and improve sleep.

Impact of Illicit Drugs on Sleep:
- **Stimulants:** increase wakefulness and reduce total sleep time and REM sleep.
- **Depressants:** may initially promote sleep but disrupt sleep architecture, leading to fragmented sleep and reduced REM sleep.
- **Cannabis:** can help with sleep onset, but chronic use may alter sleep stages, reducing REM sleep and impairing cognitive functions.

Promoting Mental Health Through Better Sleep

Maintaining a Regular Sleep Schedule
A consistent sleep schedule is crucial for regulating the circadian rhythm and improving sleep quality. Going to bed and waking up at the same time every day, even on weekends, helps stabilize the internal clock and promote better sleep.

Creating a Relaxing Bedtime Routine
Establishing a relaxing bedtime routine can signal to the body that it is time to wind down and prepare for sleep. Activities such as reading, taking a warm bath, or practising relaxation techniques can help reduce stress and promote relaxation.

Using Relaxation Techniques
Relaxation techniques, including deep breathing exercises, progressive muscle relaxation, and mindfulness meditation, can help reduce stress and anxiety, making it easier to fall asleep and stay asleep. Incorporating these techniques into a nightly routine can improve sleep quality and mental health.

Optimising the Sleep Environment

Creating a sleep-friendly environment is essential for promoting good sleep. This includes maintaining a cool, dark, and quiet room, using comfortable bedding, and minimizing disruptions from noise and light. Keeping electronic devices out of the bedroom and limiting screen time before bed can also enhance sleep quality.

Addressing Underlying Mental Health Conditions

Effectively managing underlying mental health conditions, such as depression, anxiety, and PTSD, is crucial for improving sleep. This may involve a combination of therapy, medication, and lifestyle changes. Addressing these conditions can lead to significant improvements in sleep quality and overall well-being.

The Role of Medication in Sleep and Mental Health

Antidepressants

Certain antidepressants, such as selective serotonin reuptake inhibitors (SSRIs) and tricyclic antidepressants (TCAs), can have both positive and negative effects on sleep. While some may improve sleep by alleviating depressive symptoms, others can cause insomnia or sedation. It is important to work closely with a healthcare provider to find the right medication and dosage.

Anxiolytics: Impact on Sleep and Usage Guidelines

Medications used to treat anxiety, such as benzodiazepines and non-benzodiazepine hypnotics, can help improve sleep by reducing anxiety and promoting relaxation. While these medications can be effective in the short term, they carry risks of dependency and tolerance, making them suitable for short-term use only. Understanding the impact of these medications on sleep architecture is crucial for managing their use and mitigating potential side effects.

Benzodiazepines

Benzodiazepines, such as temazepam and diazepam, are commonly prescribed for anxiety and insomnia. They work by enhancing the effect of the neurotransmitter GABA, which promotes relaxation and reduces anxiety.

- **Impact on Sleep Architecture**: Benzodiazepines increase the amount of time spent in stage 2 non-REM sleep but decrease the duration of slow-wave sleep (stage 3) and REM sleep. This alteration in sleep architecture can impair restorative sleep and cognitive functions.
- **Risks**: Prolonged use of benzodiazepines can lead to dependency and tolerance, where higher doses are needed to achieve the same effects. This can make discontinuation difficult, with potential withdrawal symptoms including rebound insomnia and increased anxiety.
- **Short-Term Use**: Due to these risks, benzodiazepines are generally recommended for short-term use. They can be effective for acute anxiety and temporary sleep disturbances, but long-term management should involve other treatments such as cognitive behavioral therapy (CBT).

Non-Benzodiazepine Hypnotics

Non-benzodiazepine hypnotics, such as zolpidem and eszopiclone, are also used to treat anxiety-related insomnia. These medications are often referred to as "Z-drugs."

- **Mechanism of Action**: Non-benzodiazepine hypnotics work similarly to benzodiazepines by enhancing GABA activity, promoting relaxation and sleep.
- **Impact on Sleep Architecture**: While these medications can help with sleep onset and maintenance, they also tend to decrease REM sleep and may affect the duration of slow-wave sleep. This can lead to less restorative sleep over time.
- **Risks**: Like benzodiazepines, non-benzodiazepine hypnotics can lead to dependency and tolerance with prolonged use. They are also associated with side effects such as dizziness, headache, and daytime drowsiness.
- **Short-Term Use**: These medications are typically recommended for short-term use to avoid dependency and tolerance. They can be beneficial for managing acute sleep disturbances related to anxiety.

Guidelines for Use

- **Short-Term Solution**: Both benzodiazepines and non-benzodiazepine hypnotics should be used as short-term solutions for managing anxiety-related sleep disturbances. They are effective in reducing anxiety and promoting sleep but are not suitable for long-term use due to the risk of dependency and tolerance.
- **Monitoring and Review**: Regular monitoring and medication reviews are essential when using these medications to ensure they are used safely and effectively. Adjustments may be needed to minimize side effects and prevent dependency.
- **Combination with Non-Pharmacological Interventions**: Combining these medications with non-pharmacological interventions such as cognitive behavioral therapy for insomnia (CBT-I), relaxation techniques, and improved sleep hygiene can enhance their effectiveness and reduce the need for long-term medication use.

Anxiolytics, including benzodiazepines and non-benzodiazepine hypnotics, can provide significant relief from anxiety and improve sleep in the short term. However, their impact on sleep architecture, particularly the reduction in REM and slow-wave sleep, along with the risks of dependency and tolerance, limit their suitability for long-term use. A comprehensive approach that includes non-pharmacological interventions and regular monitoring can help manage anxiety-related sleep disturbances effectively while minimizing potential risks.

Antipsychotics

In some cases, antipsychotic medications may be prescribed to manage severe sleep disturbances associated with mental health conditions such as schizophrenia or bipolar disorder. These medications can help stabilize mood and improve sleep, but they also come with potential side effects that need to be monitored.

Effects of Olanzapine and Quetiapine on Sleep

Olanzapine and Quetiapine: These antipsychotic medications generally increase slow-wave sleep (SWS), contributing to deeper and more restorative sleep. They also reduce REM sleep duration and delay its onset, which can influence emotional and cognitive functions. While these effects improve overall sleep quality, the potential long-term impacts on REM sleep require careful consideration.

Light Therapy Boxes

Light Therapy Boxes: These devices emit bright light that mimics natural sunlight. They are used to treat seasonal affective disorder (SAD) and other conditions where exposure to natural light is limited. Light therapy boxes can be particularly beneficial for individuals in regions with long winters and short days, such as northern Scandinavia. However, sky gazing is often more effective due to the natural spectrum and intensity of sunlight.

Benefits and Usage: light therapy boxes can help reset the circadian rhythm, improve mood, and enhance alertness. They are typically used for 20-30 minutes in the morning to simulate sunlight exposure

Conclusion

The relationship between sleep and mental health is complex and bidirectional, with each influencing the other. Addressing sleep disturbances through a combination of behavioural, cognitive, and pharmacological interventions can significantly improve mental health outcomes. Health professionals play a critical role in identifying and treating sleep issues in individuals with mental health conditions, promoting better sleep and overall well-being. By prioritizing sleep health and integrating evidence-based strategies, we can enhance both mental health and quality of life.

Chapter 9: Sleep in Special Populations

Sleep in Older Adults

Changes in Sleep Patterns

As people age, they often experience changes in sleep patterns, including earlier bedtimes and wake times, reduced deep sleep, and increased awakenings during the night. These changes can be attributed to alterations in circadian rhythms, decreased production of sleep-promoting hormones like melatonin, and the presence of chronic health conditions.

Common Sleep Disorders in Older Adults

As people age, they are more likely to experience a range of sleep disorders, including insomnia, sleep apnea, restless leg syndrome (RLS), and periodic limb movement disorder (PLMD). Addressing these conditions through appropriate interventions, such as medication, lifestyle changes, and sleep hygiene practices, can significantly improve sleep quality for older adults.

Insomnia

Insomnia is a common sleep disorder characterized by difficulty falling asleep, staying asleep, or waking up too early and not being able to go back to sleep. In older adults, insomnia can be caused by various factors including chronic medical conditions, medications, stress, and lifestyle changes. Cognitive Behavioral Therapy for Insomnia (CBT-I) is often effective in treating insomnia by addressing the underlying psychological and behavioral factors.

Sleep Apnea

Sleep apnea, particularly obstructive sleep apnea (OSA), is prevalent in older adults. OSA is characterized by repeated interruptions in breathing during sleep due to the collapse of the airway. This condition leads to fragmented sleep and reduced oxygen levels in the blood. Continuous Positive Airway Pressure (CPAP) therapy is the most effective treatment for OSA, helping to keep the airway open and improve sleep quality.

Restless Leg Syndrome (RLS) and Periodic Limb Movement Disorder (PLMD)

RLS is a condition characterised by an uncontrollable urge to move the legs, often accompanied by uncomfortable sensations. PLMD involves involuntary limb movements during sleep, leading to frequent awakenings and disrupted sleep. Both conditions are more common in older adults and can be managed with medications, lifestyle changes, and improved sleep hygiene.

Reduced Slow Wave Sleep in Aging

As people age, their ability to initiate and maintain slow wave sleep (SWS) diminishes. SWS, also known as deep sleep, is crucial for physical restoration and cognitive function. This reduction in SWS can lead to fragmented sleep and decreased overall sleep quality.

- **Accelerated Reduction in Alzheimer's Disease**: in individuals with Alzheimer's disease, the ability to initiate and maintain SWS is further compromised. This reduction in SWS exacerbates the progression of Alzheimer's, creating a vicious cycle where poor sleep quality accelerates cognitive decline, which in turn leads to even worse sleep quality.
- **Interventions and Future Developments**: devices are being developed to promote and initiate SWS, potentially offering new treatments for improving sleep quality in older adults and those with Alzheimer's. These devices, which may become available within the next five to ten years, aim to enhance the depth and duration of SWS, thereby improving overall sleep quality and cognitive health.

Addressing Sleep Disorders in Older Adults

To manage sleep disorders in older adults, a comprehensive approach that includes medication, lifestyle changes, and sleep hygiene practices is essential.

- **Medications**: depending on the specific sleep disorder, medications such as sleep aids, RLS medications, or CPAP therapy for sleep apnea may be prescribed.
- **Lifestyle Changes**: reducing caffeine and alcohol intake can improve sleep quality.
- **Establishing a Regular Sleep Schedule**: maintaining consistent sleep and wake times can help regulate circadian rhythms.
- **Optimising the Sleep Environment**: ensuring a comfortable sleep environment with minimal noise and light disruptions can enhance sleep quality.
- **Managing Chronic Conditions**: effectively managing chronic health conditions, such as arthritis, heart disease, and diabetes, can reduce sleep disruptions.

- **Promoting Physical Activity**: regular physical activity can improve sleep quality and overall health, but it should be timed appropriately to avoid stimulating effects close to bedtime.

Sleep in Shift Workers

Circadian Rhythm Disruption

Shift work can significantly disrupt the circadian rhythm, leading to difficulties in falling asleep, staying asleep, and achieving restorative sleep. Shift workers are at higher risk for sleep disorders, fatigue, and associated health problems.

Strategies for Managing Shift Work-Related Sleep Disturbances

- **Light Therapy**: exposure to bright light during work hours and avoiding light exposure during the day can help reset the circadian rhythm.
- **Sleep Scheduling**: creating a consistent sleep schedule, even on days off, can help regulate the internal clock.
- **Sleep Environment Optimisation**: using blackout curtains, white noise machines, and maintaining a cool, quiet room can improve sleep quality during the day.
- **Napping**: strategic napping can help mitigate sleep deprivation and improve alertness during work hours.

Importance of Sleep for Performance and Recovery

Adequate sleep is essential for athletes to achieve optimal performance, facilitate recovery, and maintain overall health. Sleep plays a critical role in muscle repair, cognitive function, and immune system support. Chronic sleep deprivation can impair athletic performance, increase the risk of injuries, and hinder recovery.

Effects of Sleep Deprivation on Athletes

Chronic sleep deprivation can have detrimental effects on athletic performance and overall health:

- **Impaired Performance**: lack of sleep can reduce strength, power, and endurance. It also negatively impacts coordination, accuracy, and reaction times, all of which are critical for athletic performance.
- **Increased Risk of Injuries**: sleep deprivation can lead to decreased alertness and slower reaction times, increasing the likelihood of accidents and injuries during training and competition.
- **Hindered Recovery**: inadequate sleep delays the recovery process, leading to prolonged muscle soreness and fatigue. This can reduce training efficiency and overall athletic progress.

Role of Sleep in Athletic Performance

1. **Muscle Repair and Growth**: during sleep, especially during slow-wave sleep (SWS), the body releases growth hormone, which is crucial for muscle repair and growth. Adequate sleep helps muscles recover from the stress of exercise, reducing the risk of injury and improving strength and endurance.
2. **Cognitive Function**: sleep is essential for cognitive processes such as attention, learning, memory consolidation, and decision-making. For athletes, sharp cognitive function is necessary for strategic thinking, reaction times, and overall game performance. Sleep disturbances can impair these cognitive abilities, leading to poor performance.

3. **Immune System Support**: sleep supports the immune system by promoting the production of cytokines, proteins that fight infection and inflammation. A strong immune system helps athletes recover faster from illnesses and reduces the risk of infections that can impair training and performance.

Strategies for Optimal Sleep

To enhance performance and recovery, athletes should adopt strategies that promote good sleep hygiene and align with their chronotype:

- **Consistent Sleep Schedule**: maintain a regular sleep schedule, going to bed and waking up at the same time every day, including weekends.
- **Sleep Environment**: create a conducive sleep environment by keeping the bedroom cool, dark, and quiet. Use comfortable bedding and limit exposure to screens before bedtime.
- **Relaxation Techniques**: incorporate relaxation techniques such as deep breathing, meditation, or gentle stretching to wind down before bed.
- **Nutrition and Hydration**: avoid heavy meals, caffeine, and alcohol close to bedtime. Staying hydrated and consuming a balanced diet supports overall health and sleep quality.
- **Napping**: short naps (20-30 minutes) can help alleviate daytime sleepiness and boost performance, especially for those who have had insufficient nighttime sleep.

Chronotypes: Larks and Owls

Individual differences in sleep patterns, known as chronotypes, can influence the best time for peak physical performance. Chronotypes describe whether a person is a morning type (lark) or an evening type (owl).

Larks (Morning Types)

- **Peak Performance Time**: larks typically perform best in the early to mid-morning hours. Their physical and cognitive functions are at their peak shortly after waking, making morning workouts and competitions ideal for them.
- **Sleep Patterns**: larks tend to wake up early and go to bed early. Ensuring they get adequate sleep by maintaining a consistent sleep schedule that aligns with their natural rhythm is crucial for optimal performance and recovery.

Owls (Evening Types)

- **Peak Performance Time**: owls generally perform better in the late afternoon and evening. Their energy levels and cognitive functions peak later in the day, making evening training sessions and competitions more suitable.
- **Sleep Patterns**: owls tend to wake up later and go to bed later. Allowing them to follow their natural sleep patterns and ensuring they get enough rest is important for maximizing their athletic potential.

Sleep in Pregnant Women

Sleep Disruptions During Pregnancy

Pregnancy can cause sleep disturbances due to physical discomfort, hormonal changes, and increased frequency of urination. Common sleep issues during pregnancy include insomnia, restless leg syndrome, and sleep apnea.

Strategies for Improving Sleep During Pregnancy

- **Using Supportive Pillows**: using body pillows or wedge pillows can help alleviate physical discomfort and improve sleep posture.
- **Maintaining a Consistent Sleep Schedule**: keeping regular sleep and wake times can help regulate circadian rhythms.
- **Practising Relaxation Techniques**: deep breathing exercises, prenatal yoga, and meditation can reduce stress and promote relaxation.
- **Managing Nutrition**: eating a balanced diet and avoiding heavy meals, caffeine, and sugary foods close to bedtime can improve sleep quality.

Conclusion

Sleep needs and challenges vary significantly across different populations, including older adults, shift workers, athletes, and pregnant women. Understanding these unique needs and implementing tailored strategies can enhance sleep quality and overall well-being. Health professionals play a crucial role in identifying sleep issues and providing personalised interventions to support healthy sleep habits. By addressing the specific sleep needs of special populations, we can promote better health outcomes and improve quality of life.

Chapter 10: Future Directions in Sleep Research

Emerging Trends in Sleep Medicine

Personalised Medicine

Personalised medicine is an emerging trend in sleep medicine that involves tailoring treatments to individual patients based on their genetic, environmental, and lifestyle factors. This approach can lead to more effective and targeted interventions for sleep disorders, improving patient outcomes.

Advancements in Sleep Tracking Technology

Innovations in sleep tracking technology, including wearable devices, smart home systems, and advanced sleep monitoring tools, are providing more accurate and comprehensive data on sleep patterns. These technologies can help identify sleep issues, monitor treatment progress, and offer personalised recommendations for improving sleep quality.

Novel Therapies for Sleep Disorders

Researchers are exploring new therapies for sleep disorders, including pharmacogenomics, which involves using genetic information to guide medication choices. Other promising therapies include transcranial magnetic stimulation (TMS) and cognitive behavioural therapy delivered through digital platforms.

The Role of Genetics in Sleep

Genetic Research and Sleep Patterns

Genetic research is uncovering how genes influence sleep patterns and predisposition to sleep disorders. Understanding the genetic basis of sleep can lead to personalised treatments and preventive strategies tailored to individual genetic profiles.

Potential for Personalised Sleep Medicine

Personalised sleep medicine, guided by genetic information, can improve the accuracy of diagnoses and the effectiveness of treatments. By identifying genetic markers associated with sleep disorders, healthcare providers can develop customised treatment plans that address the unique needs of each patient.

Innovations in Sleep Therapy

Transcranial Magnetic Stimulation (TMS)

TMS is a non-invasive brain stimulation technique that uses magnetic fields to stimulate nerve cells in the brain. It is being explored as a treatment for various sleep disorders, including insomnia and depression-related sleep disturbances. Early research suggests that TMS may improve sleep quality and reduce symptoms of sleep disorders.

Cognitive Behavioural Therapy (CBT) Delivered Digitally

Digital platforms are making cognitive behavioural therapy (CBT) more accessible to individuals with sleep disorders. Online CBT programs, mobile apps, and telehealth services provide convenient and cost-effective ways to deliver CBT, which has been proven effective for treating insomnia and other sleep issues.

The Future of Sleep Health

Integrating Lifestyle Modifications

Future approaches to sleep health will likely emphasise the importance of lifestyle modifications, such as diet, exercise, and stress management, in promoting better sleep. Integrating these factors into comprehensive treatment plans can enhance the effectiveness of interventions and improve overall well-being.

Technological Advancements

Technological advancements, including AI-powered sleep analysis, smart home integration, and advanced sleep tracking devices, will continue to play a crucial role in sleep health. These innovations can provide personalised insights, monitor progress, and offer targeted recommendations for improving sleep quality.

Holistic Approach to Sleep Health

A holistic approach to sleep health involves considering all aspects of an individual's life, including physical, mental, and emotional well-being. By addressing the underlying causes of sleep issues and promoting healthy lifestyle habits, healthcare providers can help patients achieve optimal sleep and overall health.

Conclusion

The future of sleep research and medicine is promising, with emerging trends and innovations offering new possibilities for diagnosing and treating sleep disorders. Personalised medicine, genetic research, and advanced sleep tracking technologies are paving the way for more targeted and effective interventions. By integrating lifestyle modifications, leveraging technological advancements, and adopting a holistic approach to sleep health, we can improve sleep quality and overall well-being for individuals worldwide. Health professionals will play a critical role in guiding these advancements and ensuring that patients receive the best possible care for their sleep needs.